Praise for *All You'll See Is Sky*

"In this exquisitely written memoir, [...] suspenseful tale capturing what it me[...] the grit that confronts all of us."
   —Stephanie Raffelock, editor of *Art in the Time of Unbearable Crisis* and author of *A Delightful Little Book On Aging* and *Creatrix Rising*

"Vivid, raw in its candor, and sensitive to the broad diversity of cultures and people, *All You'll See is Sky* takes us on a life-changing journey in Africa. This memoir is rich with the beauty of the continent—the roaring grunts of hippos, the diesel fumes, the sandstorms. It speaks profound truths about responsibility and compassion, intimacy and connection."
   —Marlena Maduro Baraf, author of *At the Narrow Waist of the World* and coauthor of *Three Poets/Tres Poetas*

"With honesty and humility, Janet A. Wilson takes the reader on a roller coaster ride through Africa, with all the sights, sounds, and history of a very complex continent. Set against the beautiful backdrop of the land and the people of Africa, *All You'll See is Sky* is a gripping and enjoyable read."
   —Vicki Cody, author of *Army Wife* and *Fly Safe*

"Janet's prose is clear, rich, and from the heart, and opens a window into another world. She shares a deep immersion into the beauty and power of the African wilderness and culture, and exposes the complicated and emotional knot of what constitutes a true partnership."
   —Annie Chappell, author of *Away Up The North Fork: A Girl's Search for Home in the Wilderness*

All You'll See Is Sky

All You'll See Is Sky

Resetting a Marriage on an Adventure Through Africa

Janet A. Wilson

SHE WRITES PRESS

Published 2024
Printed in the United States of America
Print ISBN: 978-1-64742-644-6
E-ISBN: 978-1-64742-645-3
Library of Congress Control Number: 2023911766

For information, address:
She Writes Press
1569 Solano Ave #546
Berkeley, CA 94707

Interior Design by Kiran Spees

She Writes Press is a division of SparkPoint Studio, LLC.

For my husband, Tom Feuchtwanger,
and our sons, Derek and David

Contents

Chapter 1

When Lives Collide

Calgary, Canada, 2005

In February 2005, twenty-five years after my husband, Tom, and I had immigrated from South Africa to Canada, I stood at our kitchen window and watched the crisp winter sun set over the snowy Rocky Mountains. Though the sight was beautiful, my mind was elsewhere— thousands of miles away—in a place where that same sun would rise a few hours later to illuminate the golden dunes of the Sahara Desert and filter its warm beams through the tangled jungle of the Central African rainforests.

I glanced at my watch. It was 5:53 p.m. Tom would be home from work any minute, but the minutes couldn't pass quickly enough. The sound of my breathing broke the stillness, and my heart thumped against my chest. No matter how many times I ran through the what-ifs in my mind, I just couldn't be sure what to expect from the significant, life-altering change I was about to set in motion. But I knew there would be no turning back. My decision had been made.

I heard the crack and then the whining hum of the garage door opening, and Tom's black SUV roared into the garage. Moments later, he opened the back door, as he had done every workday for the thirty-five years of our marriage, and yelled, "Hi, I'm home."

His well-worn brown leather briefcase hit the floor with a thud. He turned, hung up his black suit jacket in the entrance closet, and removed his shoes before loosening his tie—his corporate noose, as I called it. I stood still and watched his every move. He walked toward

1

me to hug me. But I could no longer consider it as anything other than an empty embrace.

I stood rigid, my arms frozen at my sides, and blurted out, "We need to talk. I've got something to tell you."

Tom stepped back, and his amber eyes flickered, scanning my face for answers. Anxious and determined not to be sidetracked, I turned and walked out of the kitchen. He followed without a word, the sound of his footsteps behind me like a heavy drumbeat. I sat down on the sofa, and Tom lowered himself into the easy chair opposite. For several seconds, I looked at my husband closely, a man who seemed to have everything, a successful businessman and a good father. But the change I was determined to put into motion didn't depend on him.

Even so, I wasn't as composed as I had planned to be. All of a sudden, my words just tumbled forth. "I want out of this life. I can't keep on like this. I just can't."

I closed my eyes as if wanting to make Tom disappear. When I opened them again, I saw that he had remained motionless. Seconds passed, and still, he said nothing. Almost in desperation, afraid I'd lose my advantage or my will if I waited too long, I forced myself to continue.

"Today, I asked myself, if I had one year to live, what would I do? And I decided"—the words gushed out as if already on a journey—"I'm going to drive the length of Africa, from Cape Town to Cairo."

Tom looked at me without blinking. The muscles around his mouth twitched. He leaned forward and rested his elbows on his knees.

His voice trembled. "You're leaving me?"

I shifted on the sofa, not sure if leaving him was my only intention. Somehow, it was primarily my decision to return to Africa, and not just the state of our relationship, that urgently drove me forward.

His eyes pierced through me. "Why are you doing this?" he said with an edge to his voice.

I swallowed hard and fought to keep my composure. "I'm not really sure. I guess I want to do more with my life. It feels . . ." I struggled to find the right word. "Empty."

"What about your job?"

"I'll resign or . . . I'll ask for a leave of absence."

Tom scowled. "Those are developing countries you're talking about. What if something happened to you on the drive? What if you died down there?"

His resistance, interestingly enough, gave me courage. "I can't stop living because I'm afraid of dying." Even as I spoke, I began to feel stronger and more alive. "I'm past fifty now. I've got to do this while I still can."

Tom leaned back in his chair and let out a sigh. Then he stood up and walked toward me. So, without hesitation, I got up, and he took me in his arms. With no word spoken, he held me tightly, each of us deep in our thoughts, masking our fears and confusion. At that instant, I knew, one way or another, that nothing would ever be the same again.

I had chosen Africa for my life-changing midlife journey because Tom and I had been born and raised there. As a young couple, we had lived in the wilderness with our firstborn son, Derek, who played under a variety of wild mopane, acacia, and fever trees while the monkeys chattered and frolicked above. I loved the wilderness, the smell of the earth after the thunderstorms that rolled across the bushveld in the afternoons, the sounds of the branches snapping as buck walked past, the call of the hyenas and bush babies in the evening, the raucous call of the hadeda ibis in the morning. When the military called up Tom and told him he had to report for duty, and I was pregnant with our second son, David, we made our big decision. We were no longer willing to support the brutal system of apartheid with our presence, so we had to leave South Africa. Convinced of the rightness of our plans, we packed up and moved to Canada. In some powerful sense, my midlife decision to return home was completing a natural cycle.

Lengthy discussion filled the days following my announcement of my decision to drive the length of Africa, as Tom and I shredded and analyzed our lives. He struggled to understand my need to give up everything we had, everything we had worked for, and my choice to walk out of our lives into an unknown future. All of our assumptions were challenged—about our marriage, our relationship, our retirement, and our future together, everything about us. We argued, and I cried, the questions endless and the answers elusive.

Days later, as Tom sipped his morning coffee, he asked, "If I join you, what the hell will we do with the house?"

"I don't care about the house." I looked out the window to the view of the mountains in the distance. "You can sell it. I want out of our lifestyle."

"What about Derek and David? How will they feel?"

I felt that familiar mother's guilt well up in me. What would they say? They lived their own lives now. Indeed, they no longer needed me. I glanced up at their photographs on the mantel. Smiling faces on the ski hill. Would they even miss me?

"They don't need me anymore. They'll be fine." I hesitated. "I think they'd want me to do something for myself now."

"Just how do you suppose you're going to pay for this? The cost would use up all our retirement savings."

"I'll eat peanut butter sandwiches for the rest of my life if I have to, but I'm going. I'm leaving." I had no firm idea where all my frustration and restlessness was coming from, but the emotions lit a spark of energy in me, an energy to chase what I wanted.

We wrapped our nights together for two weeks in words of fury, rage, distress, and heartbreak. All the constant arguing pulled me in two directions—my heart screaming to leave, and yet my head telling me not to make a decision I would later regret.

The days and nights crept on. One evening I sat on the edge of our bed. Tom lay there listening to music, his ears covered with his headphones. He had shut me out. I hadn't drawn the drapes, and the blackness of the night outside filled me with dread.

"Tom." I shook him to get his attention. "I can't live like this anymore." Even my sighing now felt like nausea. "Everything's so controlled, so predictable. I feel as if every day I'm on replay." The truth was that I had begun to drown in a sea of safety and security, and I simply could not live a moment longer according to society's packaged lifestyle and its expectations of who I should be. Every minute of every day, I struggled to understand the emptiness I felt. I had everything I could ask for, everything western civilization had promised, and yet I felt trapped behind an invisible wall.

Tom could not grasp my position. His confusion made him defensive. "I've sacrificed so much and worked so damn hard to give you everything you need. What more do you want from me?"

It seemed that some kind of existential quicksand was pulling me down into a dark void. Desperately seeking some explanation for my feelings, I blamed his work.

"You sold out completely to the corporate world. You're chasing the wrong dreams."

His jaw dropped open, but whatever thoughts were racing through his mind didn't develop into words. Finally, he just said wearily, "I don't know how to be in your life anymore." Shaking his head, he got up and walked away.

"This is my time," I said to his retreating back. "I need to do what I want, not what the family wants, not what society demands of me or what your damn career needs."

He abruptly turned around. "Stop yelling at me."

"I'm not yelling." But I was. I got up and walked out of the house into the darkness. The cold Canadian air bit into me as the snow crunched beneath my boots. For the thousandth time, I wondered if I was strong enough to carry out my plan.

I thought of the years of marriage and individual therapy we both had struggled through. Therapy had thrown us life jackets, and we were no longer drowning, but to truly save myself or our marriage, we still had to swim to shore. The issue now was that I wasn't sure I could even see us standing together on that shore, nor did I feel the same need to reach it, at least not as a couple. For me, our relationship had reached the tipping point, beyond which lay only one clear idea: my return to Africa. And yet I wasn't giving up on the idea of our marriage either. We both had long ago accepted our flaws. Tom admitted that his ambitions had caused conflict and that he often made decisions about what we needed, even when it was not what I wanted. I accepted that I had become the complicit domestic: keeping the home front and caring for our sons while he achieved his career aspirations. My dreams and goals had been put on hold until now. I now understood that I was no longer willing to let him determine my life and that I was finally ready, at any cost, to take charge of my destiny. I was prepared to power through to shore no matter how choppy the waves might be or whether I would ultimately have to stand alone on those sands. But still, the decision was heart-wrenching.

I lay in bed after another restless night. Tom's head, with his untamed thick brown hair, rested on the pillow beside me. He let out a soft snore and turned over. He looked peaceful. I wondered if he would be by my side forever or whether we would soon go our separate ways.

Now, lying beside him, I thought that maybe I still loved him, but I knew that love—when it was merely going through its paces—wasn't enough. There had to be more to my life, but I was unsure what would give my existence more meaning. Africa, however, remained a certainty. For mysterious reasons I had yet to explore, the idea of Africa had been a shining beacon to me for many years.

Tom opened his eyes and reached out to touch my arm, his hand warm and gentle. I felt a knot of sadness in my throat.

"I can't change your mind, can I?" he asked.

"No, Tom. I'm sorry," I whispered.

He turned to face me, propping himself up on his left elbow. An uneasy silence hung in the air for a few seconds; then he let out a deep sigh. "I'll come with you. Let's do it."

I sat up and looked at him, surprised. While it was reassuring to know that he would bring his skills and knowledge to the journey, I nevertheless felt anxious. Did I want to risk sharing my dream with him? After all, his dreams and ambitions had become my prison. I, the loving and supportive wife (oh, how I hated that cliché), had helped build and support them at the cost of mine. Would he now live in my shadow, as I had lived in his? Would he become the invisible partner in our marriage? Was there enough space in our relationship for both of our dreams and ambitions?

My body stayed tense, but I spoke as calmly as possible. "What made you change your mind?"

He lay back down on the bed, his gaze fixed on me. There was an air of reticence about him that I hadn't noticed before. He reached out, and I felt his firm grip on my arm.

"I don't want to lose you." He gently pulled me back down, and we held each other in a moment of silence. But the hours that followed were fitful for me; I simply didn't know whether Tom's decision was a positive change or even whether I wanted him to come with me.

The morning light greeted our new day. Tom slipped out of bed, and as I listened to the clatter in the kitchen, I breathed in the scent of freshly brewed coffee, my thoughts wildly out of sync with the familiar routine.

Tom returned with the coffee and toast. "We'll start planning this weekend."

I nodded my head. But I was thinking, *This is my journey, Tom. My time. If I let you come along, things will have to be different.*

In the meantime, I saw no harm in letting others know about our intentions. To my surprise, however, my decision to drive from Cape Town to Cairo was met with disbelief, ridicule, horror stories, and almost no words of encouragement. Our families, friends, and colleagues thought we were reckless to risk so much, and some predicted that we wouldn't make it. Our son Derek asked why we didn't just play golf like the rest of our friends. Of course, I understood some of their apprehensions. Our route, estimated at over twenty thousand miles, would take us often through remote, harsh, and sparsely inhabited places and some areas with security concerns. Just the list of vaccinations required was enough to stop many of our friends, family, and colleagues from leaving Canada.

But despite the lack of enthusiasm from others, we went ahead and set a potential departure date, even though I felt that Tom was still on trial. As our planning entered the serious stage, my concerns increased. While Tom's support was helpful, it soon became evident that planning the trip was a microcosm of our relationship.

As I entered his office one afternoon, he pointed to his work area.

"Look," he said. "I've got the plan outline."

I glanced at the spreadsheet glowing from his computer screen, his to-do lists neatly stacked on his desk, a financial budget outlined, and maps taped to the wall.

"We're all set to start." He smiled as he spoke, obviously pleased with himself.

I winced inwardly. This just wasn't going to work. I no longer wanted Tom to determine everything in my life, our lives. If we couldn't get through this planning stage of the trip as equal partners, getting all the way to Cairo together would be impossible.

"Okay," I said, putting off the confrontation momentarily and turning and going back upstairs.

Once there, I thought of all I had given up for him, my whole identity, even my name. In fairness, I couldn't say he'd been unkind to me or that he'd ever neglected our sons, or that he'd failed to be a good provider. But he had made every big decision in our lives, and the resentment I felt over this was painful. And now he wanted to take over my dream to drive through Africa. We had arrived at our first roadblock. There was no way to avoid the inevitable: I had to tell him that our old way of doing things was finally over.

Chapter 2

Drowning in a Sea of Information

Calgary, Canada, February 2005

I was working as a nurse in psychiatry, and every day I heard the patients' cries of regrets, their pain of living unfulfilled lives, and their urges to die rather than to live with that pain. While my situation was neither so dire nor so dramatic, I realized that the difference was only in degree and not in kind. After all, no one wants to carry the burden of regret and guilt for not acting when action is most required. We all want fulfillment and peace according to our individual terms and circumstances.

Two years earlier, I had moved from palliative care to psychiatry: from the struggles of those who do not want to die to the struggles of those who do. I thought of the patients who had touched my life, the patients whose hands I had held as they took their last breaths. I thought of Trevor, of Marilyn, of Annie. I especially thought of Annie.

I remembered how we had watched and waited, waited for the young woman to die. Her skin looked transparent in the soft daylight that streamed through the open window as if caressing her in her final moments, her wisps of hair a reminder of her struggles with chemotherapy. She looked to be asleep, her breaths shallow and slow, her frailty hidden behind the youth of her body. The nurses wrapped her in warm blankets, gently held her hands, and wet her lips. We whispered soothing words to her. We waited. Then—stillness and no movement. I reached out to touch her and placed my cold stethoscope on her warm chest. I listened to the silence. Quiet filled the room as I closed her eyes and pulled the white sheet up and over her face.

Even in our presence, Annie died alone. There were no sobbing relatives, no grieving friends at her side. Forgotten before she was even dead, a life unknown, a story untold. I turned around and left the room. My footsteps echoed my dismay at another young life taken.

Back at the nursing station, I looked at the desk cluttered with papers, patient charts, computers, phones, and pens. The shelves above were packed with policy and procedure manuals and medical, diagnostic, pharmacological, and nursing textbooks. Bev, a nursing colleague, sat at the desk and sipped her tea as she read a patient's chart. She glanced up at me.

"How's Annie?" she asked.

I sat down. "Annie's gone."

Bev leaned back in her chair. "It never gets easier, does it?" She sighed. "Dr. Adams is on call. I'll page her to come in and sign the death certificate."

I opened Annie's chart: her last three weeks of life, carefully documented. Turning to the family-history section, I moved my finger down the page and stopped at "Next of Kin." Annie had a brother, Jason. I picked up the phone and dialed.

Bev pushed her glasses up her nose. "Do you know what funeral home Annie wanted us to contact?"

I shook my head. "No. Just call the funeral home next on the call list."

Then I picked up my pen and charted one last time: "No vital signs. Time of death 0906. Next of kin notified. Dr. Adams notified." It is never easy to witness a death, especially that of one so young. Annie had arrived propped up on the stretcher, a pink knitted cap—pink was her favorite color—pulled down low over her ears. At twenty-four years old, she had come to die.

At fifty-four, I was old enough to be her mother.

As I listened to the nurses' morning report on the psychiatry unit and heard again the stories of patients who fought against the urge to hurt or kill themselves, I thought of Annie and those who struggle to live. And I asked myself: *If I had one year to live, what would I do?* I knew the answer before the question had hardly left my lips. I didn't think about Tom or our marriage then, but now I did.

Like most couples, we had fallen in love when we had nothing but each other. We made love and laughed, which sparked a flame of excitement and passion in our relationship. Eventually, however, children, careers, and responsibilities gradually robbed us of time and energy together. Tom and I began to live parallel lives, checking each other's calendars and schedules to see when we could fit each other in. Intimacy slid out through the cracks in our relationship, and a busyness took its place. And this became our ordinary, at least until our sons left home, friends began to die or get divorced, and my retirement loomed on the horizon. One morning, I had looked across the kitchen table at Tom and wondered, *Who are you, Tom, and where have you been?*

Now that we had decided to leave for Africa together, I walked around the home that had become my prison—filled with furniture. The dining room table where we entertained our friends, pictures on the walls, pots and pans in the kitchen, books I had read collecting dust, the king-size bed where we infrequently made love. Nothing seemed to matter anymore.

But our marriage wasn't the only problem; the problem was also the way we had chosen to live. Above all else, I wanted to be able to view my world without the clutter that filled it, the clutter of material goods but also of control. Society's experts challenged my spirit of independence: I no longer needed to make even the most minor decisions. The nutritionist told me what to eat; fitness experts prescribed what exercises to do; physicians informed me how to manage my health; fashion designers determined what I should wear; the financial planners explained how to budget and save; the TV commercials told me what to buy; even the book reviewers recommended what to read. Everything was gobbling me up and spitting me out as a mindless consumer. And now Tom was telling me how my dream should be planned, budgeted, and organized.

I returned to the basement and sat down in the green leather recliner. "Tom," I said to get his attention. "We're going to have to do things differently." I clutched my scribbled to-do list.

He looked up from the computer. "What do you mean?" He had become a spreadsheet fiend, with every detail finding its way into a cell and a column. Working as an exploration geologist, he loved details and planning.

"There are too many decisions to be made, so we need to figure out who will do what and then accept whatever decision we each make." I sucked in the air. "You're going to have to trust my decisions completely."

Tom turned his chair around and faced me. "Of course, I trust your decisions. What makes you think I don't?"

"So, it's okay, then, if I make all the plans for dismantling our lives in Canada, and you decide on the vehicle, navigation system, and equipment?"

Why was I asking him for his permission to make a decision? I had to change as well. It wasn't all about Tom. Despite years of marriage therapy, we were still trapped in bad relationship habits. We had also drifted apart, pursuing different careers and interests, and establishing friendships that weren't mutual.

Tom looked straight at me, and then, without a word, he turned and returned to working on his plan. I took his silence as agreement.

And so, the actual planning began, our evenings spent drowning in a sea of information and a vast number of decisions to be made, with exciting speculations and frustrating arguments as we navigated through the maze of facts and figures. It no longer mattered why I'd decided to drive through Africa. It was the right choice. We pored over maps to choose our route. Africa is the world's second-largest continent, with over a billion people, fifty-four countries, and thousands of languages. Our journey up the east coast would take us through at least twelve countries.

We listed all the training required to drive safely on our own. Some, such as advanced off-road driving, would have to wait until we got to Africa, but other skills, such as wilderness and remote first aid, could be enhanced in Canada.

Excited, we headed off for our first class, but we came home with a new realization: a Canadian-wilderness first aid course wouldn't meet our needs. We couldn't, for example, "stabilize the patient until help arrived." We were the help and needed to be fully equipped and prepared to deal with anything life would throw at us. There would be no 911 emergency number to call. No search-and-rescue teams. We needed to be totally independent and utterly reliant on each other. I felt a sense of panic; I couldn't even change a flat tire.

Tom, however, had not lost the discipline of his training as a navy diver in the South African military. During the apartheid era, conscription was mandatory for eighteen-year-old white males. Tom still worked out regularly and was physically strong and healthy. He had spent his early years mapping and doing mineral exploration in the African bush. The navigation skills he'd learned had him building our own GPS-based navigation system for Africa. I would have the best navigator at my side. Although I had learned to drive off-road in Africa, having Tom's off-road-driving and vehicle-recovery expertise on board would be helpful. Combined with my medical knowledge, we had a good foundation for a capable team.

But we still faced steep learning curves in many areas. At times I felt overwhelmed, but the excitement was contagious. I also felt more alive than I had in years.

"Tom," I yelled from the basement one day, "I think I've found our Land Cruiser for sale in South Africa."

A vehicle was the most essential purchase we needed to make. Tom hurried down the stairs, and together we studied the 1997 Land Cruiser 80 Series on the computer screen.

"Perfect. Just what we're looking for," he said.

There followed a flurry of emails between an off-road-vehicle-conversion specialist in South Africa as we negotiated to purchase the Land Cruiser. With the specialist's guidance, we determined what modifications the vehicle required for a long-distance African expedition. At last, we sent the money, and the deal was sealed; now committed to the trip, we toasted to our future.

Cape Town and Cairo, here we come!

But the spreadsheet fiend continued to plan. There was no end in sight; there would always be new information and more decisions. I began to feel that Tom would plan our lives away and that we would never leave. With the Land Cruiser purchased, a friend lined up to look after our house and dogs, and Tom's consulting business deals finalized, I decided the time had come. I went to a travel agent.

"I've bought the plane tickets," I announced as I entered his office. "We're leaving for South Africa on September fourteenth."

Deep into populating one of his many spreadsheets and timelines, Tom looked up. "What! I haven't finished our planning document yet."

"You can finish the plan on the plane," I replied. "We're leaving in three weeks."

But despite my outward appearance of bravado, a wave of doubt and vulnerability swept over me. Never before had I felt so emotionally naked. Yet, at the same time, I realized I was building a new kind of protective cover—stronger, richer, and better able to shield me from the banalities of a too-predictable and overly commodified life. More than ever, the imagined African sun of my daydreams began to warm the essential part of me that I had neglected for far too long.

Chapter 3
My Childhood in South Africa

Johannesburg, South Africa, 2005

As I walked across the driveway toward the loaded car, our dogs jumped around, barking with the anticipation of coming with us. With sadness, I told them to wait for me and that I would be back. And then we left for the Calgary Airport.

Thirty-six hours after leaving, we began our descent into Johannesburg Airport, where my cousin Jenny and her husband, Bruce, met us. We would stay with them while we made our final preparations before leaving on our epic driving adventure.

When we arrived, Jenny and Bruce's several dogs greeted us, and I had a sense of both continuity and dislocation. Dogs on one continent and dogs on another, but these weren't my dogs. For just a few seconds, I wondered which continent was truly my own. No doubt, our adventure would go a long way toward an answer, and so I was even more excited than before to get started. I walked across the brick driveway past all the dogs' drinking bowls at the entrance to the house and followed Jenny into the large sunny kitchen. Immediately, I felt I had stepped back into my childhood.

A washing machine hummed into its last spin. On top of it, a pile of wet clothing waited to be hung in the sun. Two neglected plants alongside a collection of abandoned plastic containers sat on the windowsill, and an assortment of dishes stacked high, beside the sink, dried in the breeze drifting through the open burglar-barred windows. A grocery store calendar with dates circled and appointments jotted down hung beside the kitchen table. Jenny put the kettle on for tea, and the dogs settled down at our feet to sleep on the tiled floors.

Jenny is a year younger than I am. We had spent our early years growing up together in the dusty steel-and-iron industrial town of Vereeniging before her family moved away. Jenny was loved, generous, and clever. Her thick ginger hair had usually been pulled back and tamed in pigtails, and she'd always worn shoes, even when we'd played in the dirt. I couldn't recall her ever being in trouble, nor could I imagine her running away.

Vereeniging, South Africa, 1951–1969

Dogs barking and yellow weaverbirds chattering woke me up the following morning. I glanced in the mirror. My morning hair always looks as if it has been at war all night with my pillow. I inherited my mother's thin, straight hair and my father's blue eyes, but that is where the similarities end. My mother's travels in life were between our home, the library, and the church. My father's trips were even shorter—between our house and his office.

But I was born to wander and started at an early age. A rambunctious child, willful and stubborn, I thrived with the wind in my hair, the sun on my face, and the naked, dusty earth beneath my bare feet. Nature was my playground and teacher. I had an insatiable curiosity and a restless energy to match.

My mother hid behind her books and knitting. She sent me to nursery school at the age of three, an attempt to tame my unruliness and rein me in. The nursery school was located in a brick house several blocks from where I lived. After lunch each day, we had to lie down for a nap. On my fourth day, I lay on my mat and waited for the no-nonsense lady in charge to leave the room. I then got up, walked to the window, opened it, climbed out, and ran across the grass toward the low brick wall around the yard. I scrambled over the brick wall and ran home, my bare feet beating a path on the dusty road to freedom. My mother, who could read while knitting, glanced up from her book as I entered the room.

"I can't do inside," I told her.

The clicking of the needles stopped. Finally, my mother, then six months pregnant with my sister, lowered the half-finished yellow baby sweater into her lap. The defeat in her expression and tone was heavier than I'd ever experienced. She sighed, and the words seemed to slide out at the same time. "I don't know what to do with you. I simply don't know." She studied me for several long seconds as doves cooed, "*pip, pip, prrr,*" from the sneezewood tree outside her window. At last, her whole being seemed to decide something—about herself or me; it was impossible to distinguish.

She never sent me back to the nursery school, and I was free once more to roam the neighborhood. Looking back now, I realize that the only rules imposed on me as a young child were that I had to be out of my pajamas before I left the house and that I had to be home for meals.

My mother was petite. Permed brown hair framed her oval face. Tears filled her powdery blue eyes and her ivory skin turned pink when I made her angry, which was often. Although she never shouted at me (in fact, she seldom said anything), she often simply turned and walked away. Always in nylon stockings and sensible shoes, she made her dresses with the same Vogue pattern: short sleeves, buttons down the front from a little collar to her waist. Elizabeth Arden's Blue Grass perfume, with its fragrance of fresh fields of wild lavender and jasmine, was her only indulgence.

As a child, I thought all mothers were like my mother. She was kind and tried to reassure me. "There is no *tokoloshe* under your bed," she would say. But I knew she was wrong. Still, I tried not to be fearful of that evil African spirit that I was sure I heard shuffling under my bed in the dark.

I liked that my mother didn't bother me too much about what I did. When she wasn't knitting or reading, she tended her rose garden and supervised Anna, our maid, and the steady stream of nameless and anonymous Black "garden boys," men who mowed the lawn, weeded her flower beds, and pruned the fruit trees. Even though they were men, they were given the derogatory name of "garden boys" (never "gardeners") by whites; even white children, including me, called them that.

Now, when I recall those years, I realize that I never knew or understood my mother. Locked in her private world of silent obedience, she existed behind a barrier that I was never able to penetrate. She accepted whatever life offered her with a sorrowful resignation and few complaints. I remember, at the age of twelve, begging my tearful mother to leave my father. She said she couldn't leave him because of me. Well, she didn't say it in those exact words, but as a child, that's what I believed. My mother was firmly of "that generation" when being a woman meant staying home to serve her husband's needs, ironing his shirts, serving him meals, and taking care of his children. All her dreams and ambitions, whatever they might have been, were locked away, never to be achieved or even articulated.

"I should've drowned you when you were a wee pup," my father routinely told me. I entered the world as his biggest disappointment—his first child, a girl—and our relationship was a struggle from that day on. The ongoing confrontations between my father and me sculpted my views of how to be a girl in the world. In short, I believed that my life would be an ongoing battle. From those daily struggles with my father, a defiant resilience developed in me, but unfortunately, so did my inability to trust and perhaps even to love.

My father—I always called him Bob, never Dad—was an absent and disinterested parent, whereas my mother was present but often overwhelmed by the responsibilities of trying to raise daughters in a man's world. Between the two of them, they rarely told me what to do, and so I indulged my spirit of relentless inquisitiveness and passion for the outdoors and nature. Despite his general indifference, my father at least responded to my physicality. A prize boxer in his youth, he taught me how to fight, and I fought a hard fight until puberty set in, when I developed breasts as the neighborhood boys grew muscles.

Bob, an electrical engineer, was a complicated perfectionist who spoke with glares, growls, and occasional words. Even so, I thought he was strikingly handsome, with never a hair out of place and his strong-jawed face always cleanly shaven. His piercing blue eyes would slice through me, and, in his strong Scottish accent, he teased and ridiculed me at every opportunity. Fit and muscular, with powerfully built legs, his only body flaw was a large ugly scar on his right thigh. He refused to talk about it, but my mother told me it was from a wound inflicted during World War II when he served in the British air force as a ham radio operator, listening to and tapping out messages in Morse code. Stationed in India, he survived on rice for four years, so, naturally enough, we never had rice at home.

My sister Margaret entered the world as a shy, nervous creature with pale, fragile skin and hair even finer than mine. A picky eater, she had incredibly skinny legs (hardly more than bones), a small mouth, blue eyes, and a sunburned nose framed by straight blonde hair that she twirled around when she sucked her thumb. Margaret cried a lot, and I bossed her, but when the neighbor bully threw a brick at her and blood ran down her face, a rage in me made me beat the wiry boy with a fury that I found exhilarating and satisfying. I remember fiercely hoping that my father would be proud of me. But the hope was never realized in all the years of our strained relationship (which, in the end, weren't that many). In some way, perhaps, my restless nature rises out of some ceaseless and subconscious desire to impress that glowering, oppressive patriarch, but if so, that desire will always remain thwarted.

Our house, like all white people's homes, had a Black servant's quarters in the backyard. Our servant, Anna—I called her Nanna—lived in a simple brick structure, a small room with a lavatory. She had been with us since I was born and was the only Black person I knew. Nanna made my bed, polished my school shoes, ironed my school uniform, and shouted at me when I made a mess. She held me to her soft bosom when I cried. My tiny fist would clutch her soft, smooth skin, and I would breathe in the sweet smell of Sunlight soap. She ran her fingers through my hair and sang. Nanna was a second mother to me, sometimes even my first mother.

Just before my eighth birthday, I suddenly became aware of apartheid. Until that day, I had lived as any other white child growing up—playing in the sun, riding my bike, and coming home for supper—all the while accepting what I saw and heard as normal. But on March 21, 1960, I lost my childhood innocence. On that day, the Black township of Sharpeville, about eight miles from where we lived, erupted, and sixty-nine innocent Black people were massacred, shot in their backs as they ran away from the South African Police. They had been protesting peacefully against the hated pass laws. Most of those who lived in Sharpeville traveled daily in diesel-belching, overloaded Putco buses to work in Vereeniging, a town designated for whites and their Black servants who had permission to live on their employer's properties. Blacks without a permit in their passbook had to live in Sharpeville.

On the day of the massacre, my parents huddled around our kitchen table, listening to the government-owned radio station, the SABC. Voices on the radio described a different story from the one told by the voices around the table.

Bob's fury against apartheid and the Nationalist government was something to be feared. "Those bloody stupid racist Nats. They're ruining this country."

"Why did they shoot those people?" I asked.

My mother told me to leave. "This is not for children. Go outside and play."

I ran to Anna's quarters, and she let me in. "Nanna," I asked as I sat down on the cold cement floor of her room, "why did they kill the people?"

She put her head into her hands, and her wails of grief scared me. "I can take care of you but not my own child!"

I hadn't even known that she had a child.

"Elsie is same like you." Nanna held up her hand, her fingers pulled together and pointed upward, to show me that her daughter was as tall as me. She sobbed as she explained that she'd had to send her baby away. Nanna couldn't take care of her child because Elsie was not permitted to live with her mother in a white area. Apartheid had robbed Elsie of her mother and Nanna of her motherhood.

I was frightened by Nanna's angry response, but that was an important day, the day I learned the words "apartheid," "passbooks," and "racist." I was too young to understand fully what it all meant. But my friends talked about their parents, who spoke of packing up and leaving South Africa. I was confused, but I recognized that something terrible was happening. I already knew that the police were bad. They would come to our house and bang on the door, waking us up in the dark. Bob would go to the front door, and I knew my job was to go and tell Nanna and her boyfriend that the police were coming and that the boyfriend had to go to his hiding spot.

When I asked why I had to warn Nanna of the police raids, my mother would shrug and say, "You're just a child. You don't need to know these things." Nothing seemed to make sense. But that's the way it was. Without any means of learning more about these adult mysteries, I turned my attention to more straightforward childhood matters.

My passion and interest as a child were the menagerie of pets I kept in the backyard: Herbie, the tortoise that loved company. A grumpy turtle that kept escaping. Two white bunnies, Flopsy and

Mopsy, who did nothing but eat and poop. My cat Tigger had a crooked tail, and my dog Nikki had fleas (according to my mother). And in the summer, I fed my wriggling silkworms mulberry leaves from our tree in the garden. I loved GP, my guinea pig, who squealed with delight when I came home. And when my guppies had babies, I sold them to the neighborhood kids because I was saving up to buy a desk. My father refused to buy me one. He said I was stupid to think I needed a desk. "Girls are worthless," he said. My mother said nothing.

Bob occasionally drove my younger sister and me to school. As the rain thundered down on the first day of the new school year, I climbed into the car's front seat and slammed the door shut behind me.

He glanced at me as he drove. "Did you pass last year?"

"Yeah," I replied. I watched the windshield wipers fight the pouring rain.

"What grade are you going into this year?"

"Grade twelve." I was sixteen years old. In only nine months, I could leave home forever.

My father said nothing, and we relapsed into our usual silence.

In the morning, at assembly, the headmaster announced the school prefects for the new year. I came home and told my mother, "I've been made a prefect." She looked up from her knitting. "Don't be silly—who would make you a prefect?" I reached into my school bag to show her my prefect badge. She sewed it onto my blazer and never mentioned it again.

I don't remember who gave me my options, but I was told I could be a secretary, a teacher, or a nurse. As an avid reader of Arthur Mee's *The Children's Encyclopaedia*, I read and learned about geography, cultures, and other lands, which sparked a keen desire in me to explore and travel across many countries. I imagined naturally that, one day, like an explorer, I would travel all over the continent of my birth. Therefore, believing it would be my ticket to travel and work around the world, I chose nursing and midwifery. It was a decision I've always regretted. I wanted to become an explorer or work with wildlife but was told that only boys were strong and brave enough to do so.

I enrolled at the University of the Witwatersrand in Johannesburg and moved into the nurses' residence. Shortly after I arrived, I hit the party scene, and it was at a party where I first saw Tom. He was swimming in the nude and a bit drunk. Muscular and tanned, he was celebrating the completion of his mandatory military conscription and qualifications as a navy scuba diver, ready for action and duty under the command of the apartheid South African military. He swam and dove in the swimming pool like a fish. And that was how my friend Karen introduced him to me: "Meet Fish."

But it would take a year before he gathered up the courage to ask me on a date. I didn't recognize his voice over the phone, and I had forgotten that I'd met him one year previously. I told him I was busy on Saturday.

"How about Sunday?" he asked.

"Sorry, I'm busy on that night too."

"Well, when then?" He sounded slightly exasperated.

Huh, I thought, *he could be interesting.* "I can squeeze you in on Friday."

He agreed to pick me up at the student residence.

"How will I recognize you?" I asked.

But as soon I saw him, I knew he was that scuba diver who had tried to woo me one year earlier. He was different from any other guy I had gone out with, although I will admit he was a typical South African male chauvinist. He had a sense of confidence and didn't flex his muscles to try to impress me. He was funny and gentle, and he even told me that he loved the outdoors and wildlife and that his goal was to work in the bush. He also told me that he was Jewish and that his parents, to escape Hitler, had fled Germany to South Africa. As for himself, he had attended an all-boys school in Johannesburg but had difficulty fitting in. "I was a geek," he said and laughed. "I collected rocks and played the oboe in the Johannesburg junior orchestra." His rite of passage into the South African male chauvinistic community only occurred when he was called up for military service and selected for training as a navy diver. A prestigious, manly position. He was finally a jock!

I found Tom's story and his sense of humor beguiling. As a result, after our first date at a cheap Chinese restaurant, with an even cheaper bottle of Golden Dice wine, I canceled my Saturday and Sunday dates and never went out with another man.

In 1972, between studying and dodging baton-swinging police and snarling police dogs while participating in student anti-apartheid protests, Tom and I decided to get married. However, because we lived in such a male-dominated world, Tom first had to ask my father for permission to marry me.

Ignoring Tom when he entered the living room, Bob continued to read his newspaper. His big white bull terrier sat at his feet. Tom waited anxiously in the chair opposite his future father-in-law.

"Bob . . . I've something to ask you," Tom said.

Bob slowly lowered the newspaper; his dark blue eyes peered over the daily headlines. He said nothing and waited for Tom to go on.

"I want to ask you for permission to marry Janet."

"Good riddance," Bob finally said as he raised the newspaper back up and continued to read about the world. I left home and never returned.

Chapter 4
On the Banks of the iMfolozi River

South Africa, 1976-1979

After we were married, an unexpected inheritance had us setting off with backpacks on our first of many travel adventures. We spent the year exploring Europe, living in a beat-up green Renault, our first home on wheels. We got lost, scammed, robbed, attacked by gypsies, and caught in the 1974 coup in Portugal (known as the Carnation Revolution), and I got pregnant. We returned home with $30 in our pockets, the clothes we wore, no jobs, and a souvenir that changed our lives. Most people return home with a kitschy souvenir they can throw out. Not us!

Our son Derek (our souvenir conceived in Norway) was born, and Tom got a job as an exploration geologist, which sent him looking for coal in the wilderness in Zululand. No running water existed and there was certainly no electricity, but living in the wilderness stirred something in me I had never felt before: this was home; this was where I was meant to be.

We set up camp on the banks of the mighty iMfolozi River just east of the iMfolozi Game Reserve, Africa's oldest established wilderness area. At sunset, the flowers of the red-hot poker aloes glowed, and in the early hours of each day, thousands of dew-covered spider webs glistened in the morning sun. Later we set up camp at St. Lucia Wetlands (now known as the iSimangaliso Wetland Park), where large crocodiles lounged on the muddy banks while hippos floated down the river. When the hippos surfaced, they expelled a blast of air with a loud hissing sound and seemed to fart continuously. Extremely aggressive and unpredictable, hippos are reputed to kill more people every year than any other wild animal in Africa. These massive creatures—males weighing nearly one and a half tons—emerge from the water to spend the night foraging on land. Despite having short fat legs, they can reach speeds of eighteen miles an hour and will attack any person who gets in their way. "Hippo, he will bite you in half," an elderly Black man who had lived his entire life in the wilderness warned me.

At the end of every day, with Derek safely tucked in bed, Tom and I listened to the deep, roaring grunts of the hippos as they emerged from the river. As a young mother, I wasn't concerned about the hippos but worried about crocodiles, snakes, scorpions, and monkeys that lurked close to our campsite. Hordes of malaria-laden mosquitoes would take refuge in our caravan during the rainstorms, and Tom was the first to get malaria. But we forged on, learning the rules of survival in the wilds of our home continent.

No politicians lived in the area, so there were no roads. In our Land Cruiser, we bushwhacked—over hills, down valleys, across streams, and through the thornveld scrub to buy our weekly supplies from the little store in the village of Mtubatuba. Here, we met an elderly white game ranger who had lived his entire life in the African bush.

Johan wore a bashed sweat-stained hat, short khaki pants, a khaki shirt, beige socks pushed down to his ankles, and, on his feet, *veldskoen* (bush shoes) that had walked many miles over the years. Short and stocky, his skin parched by the sun and scarred by experiences, he had wild graying hair as unruly as his beard. The whole time we chatted, Johan puffed on his pipe, his blue eyes twinkling below the bushiest eyebrows I had ever seen. After we had said goodbye, Johan got into his Land Cruiser and slammed the door, which a charging buffalo had buckled. He leaned out the window and said, "Tonight, you must come for a *braai*," a barbecue. "My wife, she'll make us a nice meal."

Tom walked toward him. "Where do you stay?"

"Go this way." Johan pointed ahead. "At three miles, at the mopani tree, turn right. You'll see my tracks; just go straight. There is a river, no problem; you drive across, turn left, and go all the way until you come to my house."

"Great. We'll see you later then."

We returned to our camp, and Tom went for a shower. Our shower consisted of a wooden barrel with many small holes drilled into the bottom of it. Tom hoisted the barrel up in the tree, and our shower had a privacy screen around it made of sticks and grass. I didn't want the wildlife to see me nude! We filled the barrel with water, which created a gentle rain. After Tom emerged from the shower, he told me a boomslang snake had settled down for the winter in the privacy screen, making himself a cozy spot among the small, branch-like sticks. I refused to shower until the black-eyed green snake was gone. Boomslangs are the most venomous snake in South Africa, although not the most dangerous because they are relatively docile. But we had other creatures, such as amphibians, for company, including a giant friendly bullfrog who lived in our shower enclosure. I didn't mind sharing my shower with him though. Derek would poke the frog with a stick, and the poor creature would jump like a battery-powered toy until he smartened up and knew it was unnecessary. Eventually, Derek poked the frog but the frog didn't move. "Froggie broken," he wailed. New batteries wouldn't solve this toy problem. However, Froggie did disappear, probably becoming a meal for the boomslang in the end.

That evening we arrived at sunset at the little house of Johan and his wife, Yolandi. A cacophony of sounds always penetrates African nights in the wilderness: the high-pitched trills of cicadas, the croaking of frogs, the hooting of owls, the howling of wild jackals, and, if you're lucky, the deep roar of lions. There is never silence. Out on the porch, a light bulb, surrounded by flying bugs, lit a polished red floor littered with crash-and-burn victims. A generator hummed in the distance.

We stepped inside the two-room house, furnished with a yellow wood table, a bookcase made of planks supported by bricks, a worn sofa with two cats curled up among the cushions, two mismatched chairs, and a cluttered desk. A mammoth old yellowish elephant tusk lay in the corner. On Johan's desk, he had lined up in rows bottles of various insect specimens: scorpions, dung beetles, caterpillars, spiders, even a baboon spider, and dragonflies. Yolandi told me to keep the front door shut "to keep the snakes out." *It's a snake day*, I thought.

Johan barbequed springbok fillets, and Yolandi served potatoes, corn, and pumpkin fritters sprinkled with cinnamon. Short and well-built, Yolandi had straight hair pulled back into an untidy ponytail. She looked to be in her late fifties and slightly younger than Johan (at the time, I thought they both were ancient). Because a leopard had killed their dog in the front garden the previous week, a new puppy chewed on my bare feet under the table. Yolandi offered us rooibos tea, but I politely refused. Nanna had once told me that the tea makers didn't remove the pigeon poop mixed up with the tea leaves before they sold it, and I believed her. However, I accepted Johan's offer of "plonk," although I had no idea what was in his home brew. For all I knew, there might have been pigeon poop.

For hours Johan shared his adventures and exploits in the wilderness. He recounted hair-raising escapes and encounters with buffalos, leopards, and elephants. As I listened to his stories, I felt a strong desire to experience the freedom of the wilderness, to be held captive in the presence of an untamed Africa. I told Johan I wanted to walk through the bushveld and along the wildlife trails. He offered to arrange for a guide named Solomon to take me bush trekking in the iMfolozi Game Reserve. "He knows the bush better than anyone," he said.

Several weeks later, Tom woke me up with a cup of coffee and a rusk, a South African biscotti, before the sun was on the horizon. He planned to take Derek with him for the day, and I would spend the day with Solomon.

At the game reserve entrance, a young Black man with a rifle slung over his shoulder greeted me with a smile and a firm handshake. He also wore heavy boots: "because many snakes," he warned me. Suddenly, I experienced a flashback to my first encounter with a deadly black cobra. I was perhaps seven years old, jumping from rock to rock down a stream, when suddenly I froze with one foot in midair, as a cobra, resting on a rock I was about to step on, reared its head, flared his hood, and made a hissing sound. I froze in place on the preceding stone and, hardly breathing, watched the snake slither away. Cobras are extremely dangerous because they are nervous and aggressive, with a deadly venomous bite and spit. Once the snake was gone, I continued on my way, jumping from rock to rock.

Solomon and I set off early and walked through the bush along animal trails. Colorful butterflies flitted among the thorny acacia trees in which the playful gray vervet monkeys swung back and forth. Thousands of buffaloes, known for their savagery (they can weigh up to two thousand pounds), grazed in the distance.

"Buffalo can kill a lion," he said. He handed me his binoculars and picked up his gun. A mother warthog with three piglets, their tails held high in the air, ran by in a cloud of dust.

"I know." I raised the binoculars. "So it's a good thing I'm not a lion." I removed the binoculars. "By the way, do you get lions here?" Warthogs are wild pigs whose greatest danger comes from lions and leopards.

"Not many. Maybe if we lucky, see leopard or cheetah today."

"I want to find a white rhino," I announced with sudden passion. White rhino males weigh up to one ton and are larger than black rhinos. But they are less dangerous than their bad-tempered black cousins. A white rhino was initially called a "wijde" (meaning "wide") rhino because of its wide square lip rather than its light-gray color. The black rhino has a hook-shaped lip and is darker in color.

"I look for rhino *spore*." Solomon took a stick and, in the dirt, outlined a rhino track. "Look like this," he said, stabbing the track he had drawn.

"Where did you learn to track?"

He told me he lived with his grandparents because his mother worked for whites as a domestic in the city. He stood up, tossing the stick into the bush. I followed him through the tall grass, shrubby shrubs, and untidy trees. "My grandfather," Solomon continued, "has many cows. Every day, I look after cows since I was five. My grandfather, he teach me everything. Now I have a job." He spoke proudly. "I like it. It is better than cows."

A large herd of hundreds of grazing impalas looked up as we approached. These small bucks are the most common antelope in South Africa and are seen everywhere in the bush, so I was surprised when Solomon crouched low and waved his arm behind his back, indicating to me to get down and be quiet. Then he turned to face me. Holding his index finger to his lips, he whispered, "Shoo." I looked at the impala. "No. See there." He pointed to my left. I turned to see an elephant. "It's a girl," he said softly. She raised her trunk high, wrapped it around the fruit of a marula tree, and then swung the yellow fruit into her mouth. She did not look at us, but I was sure she knew we were there. Unconcerned, she continued to eat and flap her large ears to keep cool. I listened to the crush of leaves, sticks, and rotting fruit on the ground as she walked around the tree. A deep sense of wonder held me as I breathed in the sweet, candy-like aroma of elephant-crushed marula fruit. We stayed there for over an hour until Solomon reminded me, "We go now and look for rhino."

As we walked, I saw about ten vultures circling low in the sky. "There must be a kill below," I said. Vultures are scavengers, widely known as the eaters of the dead. Their digestion system can process large amounts of rotting flesh, and the high acidic level of their stomachs kills the pathogens. Gruesome as they seem, vultures are essential to the ecosystem balance.

Solomon chuckled. "Yes. They are like the domestic in the bush; they clean up everything."

Suddenly he stopped and bent down. "See here. Look." He pointed to a track in the soft sand. "Big rhino." I looked at the track; it was identical to what he had drawn. "Very fresh." He looked up. "He must be near." I glanced around and saw nothing. Solomon stood up slowly, looking around. "He go that way." He pointed with his rifle. "Come, we walk."

We had not walked far before I saw him. Powerful and enormous. I had never been so close to a rhino. His ears twitched, he lifted his head, and his nostrils flared. Solomon stepped back and stood beside me. "Maybe he can't see you, but he smells you and hears you very well. Stay quiet." My adrenaline pumped as the rhino trotted slowly toward us. Dust swirled around his feet. He stopped, and then, without warning, he charged. I froze. Solomon immediately stepped behind me and gripped me by my arms. He held me like a shield in front of him and the charging rhino. "Don't move," he said. The rhino barrelled down on us at full speed. Suddenly, I felt myself flying through the air. I smashed facedown into the dirt. The ground thundered and shuddered. I opened my eyes and wildly looked around. Solomon lay next to me. "You okay?" he asked. I sat up, turned around, and saw the rhino still running in the distance.

Solomon sat up. "He don't see good." He stretched out his legs in front of him and dusted off the dirt. "You stand still, and then just before rhino hit you, you jump out of his way. He passes every time."

"I'll remember that the next time I'm charged by a rhino!" I smiled with relief.

It was late when Solomon and I returned to our campsite. Tom had a fire going. In the dirt, Derek played with Tom's rock samples. As

Solomon and I sat around the fire, telling Tom about our day, a sense of sadness crept over me. I liked Solomon; I liked him a lot, and we'd had a special day together. However, when Solomon told me that his mother worked as a domestic, I had thought of Nanna and the cruelty of apartheid that could so coldly separate mothers from their children. That night by the fire, I looked at my son and could not imagine the pain of never being able or even allowed to care for him. I felt torn. I loved Africa, but I hated the brutal apartheid regime. I looked up and saw a falling star. Perhaps one day, I thought, apartheid would die just like that star. It would burn up, and all mothers would have the freedom to raise their own children. Tom and I had questioned whether we should raise our son in such an unjust country. But even though the thought of leaving Africa was painful, it could never be as excruciating as the pain of loss experienced every single moment by Black South African mothers.

After our son David was born, I knew it was only a matter of time before we left Africa. When the military called up Tom for active duty during the border war, we decided to make serious plans to leave. We wouldn't support the system of apartheid any longer. Tom flew to North America to look for a job. But after pounding the pavement in Toronto, Vancouver, Calgary, and Ann Arbor, he returned to South Africa with no job offers. Two months later, a letter from Gulf Canada arrived.

"I've got a job in Canada," Tom yelled excitedly. "We're going to Calgary."

"Calgary? Where's that?" I asked.

Tom got out an atlas, flipped the page to Canada, and put his finger on a dot. "There. That's Calgary."

I felt excited and looked forward to the adventure. However, I was concerned about the weather (I had heard it could be bitterly cold). We both agreed that it would be easier to immigrate to an English-speaking country. Tom said his career prospects would be better in

Canada, and he was also interested in working in the Arctic. I had wanted to immigrate to Australia, but Tom's decision was either Canada or the USA, so Canada it had to be.

Four months later, as we flew off the continent of Africa, I looked out of the plane window to the savannah below and promised myself, *I'll be back when apartheid's gone. Burned up like a falling star.*

But I didn't know then just how low my spirits would have to fall and burn before I'd find the courage—the courage of my wild African childhood—to begin that homeward journey.

Chapter 5
Will We Survive This Journey

Calgary, Canada, 1979

We landed in Canada, at minus twenty-two Fahrenheit, and with $3,000 in our pockets to start our lives again. Stunned by the cold, I was apprehensive, but the optimism of youth often provides the necessary courage. So, I decided to give the city a chance. We rented a small house, and Tom began his new career in oil-and-gas exploration, going to work each day in a suit and tie. He wore polished shoes, a winter jacket, gloves, and a toque. I bundled my sons in snowsuits and walked through the snow around the neighborhood. I looked forlornly at my winter boots, never realizing how much I'd miss the hot sands beneath my feet and the warm air on my skin. The icy air hit my face with such force that tears ran down my cheeks. I felt so alienated in this new world that I might as well have been in space.

Tom went to work. I bought two second-hand mattresses, which I put on the floor, and a cheap kitchen table and four chairs. I painted David's crib bright yellow. I bought pots and pans and set up our home. During supper, Tom would tell me about his exciting new life, the business associates he had met, and the people he chatted with during his day. An eerie silence hung over the long dark winter nights. I never knew the world could be so silent; no wild dogs barked, no night birds called out, and no mosquitoes buzzed. And during the days, I watched *Sesame Street* with my sons. Life appeared good, but I struggled with loneliness.

I hadn't foreseen that the transition would be so difficult. And I certainly hadn't realized how much I would miss Africa. It was as if I had left a part of myself behind, creating an emptiness that never went away. But I was determined to make our lives better. We learned to ski, toboggan, and ice-skate. I even learned to play bridge just to meet people. But I felt remote and distant. I listened to my new friends, who worried about what seemed to me irrelevant issues: weather reports, the latest fashion trends, makeup, and celebrity divorces. I tried to reassure myself that I would eventually settle down. But my angst grew every day. I thought of my mother. I had become just like her: a boring housewife, my days filled with cooking, laundry, grocery shopping, and swapping baby and children updates over a cup of coffee with friends.

With time, however, I slowly adapted to the Canadian lifestyle. We discovered the Rocky Mountains on our doorstep, which offered us a life of skiing in winter and hiking and canoeing in summer, and we soon fell in love with all that Canada offered us, especially when we began to explore the country. Our youngest son, David, had a backpack at age three, which he was expected to carry, along with his teddy bear. The first youth hostel he stayed in used to be a prison, and we stayed in a cell on the old death row. I remember reading some of the graffiti messages scribbled on the walls to my kids, not even daring to let the knowledge of apartheid's political prisoners seep through my new Canadian shield for fear of uprooting our fresh beginning right at the start.

Eventually, with my sons in school, I went to work as a nurse, hoping to fill the nagging emptiness I felt. But that was the beginning of the seduction to achieve the American dream. We learned we could have it all if we worked hard enough. So, we worked, we saved, and the chase to have it all began: safety, suburbia, status, and stuff. But like a whirlpool, the pursuit sucked us down, robbing us of time and energy; finally, it cracked our relationship.

Johannesburg, South Africa, 2005

Now, all these decades later, back on the continent of Africa, I thought about how our relationship had unraveled over the years in Canada. I wanted our old relationship back, along with my new sense of purpose and my desire to live fully and simply. But I asked myself just how much was I prepared to risk to achieve that goal.

Following our arrival in Johannesburg, Tom spent his time on the phone arranging the car insurance and the final payment needed before we could pick up our vehicle. While waiting for all the paperwork to come through, we visited the Apartheid Museum.

After parking the car in the shade of a tall blue gum tree, we walked toward the entrance of the Apartheid Museum, reflecting on the transformations of recent history and the election of President Nelson Mandela eleven years earlier. Now, with apartheid over, every South African, regardless of skin color, enjoyed the same human rights.

Buses unloaded tourists who chattered among themselves, cameras dangling around their necks and name tags pinned to their clothing. Excited children dressed in school uniforms pushed and shoved one another as they stood in line. They were not old enough to remember life under apartheid.

Teachers bellowed orders: "Get in line now." "Don't push." "Be quiet."

Tom and I had both grown up under the horrors of racism. Thousands of Black South Africans who opposed the system lost their lives, thousands more were tortured and imprisoned, thousands went into exile, and those who could fled the brutal ideology of a government gone mad. I felt ashamed as we walked past the Pillars of the Constitution—seven tall rectangular cement pillars, each featuring a word made of steel letters: "Democracy," "Equality," "Reconciliation,"

"Diversity," "Responsibility," "Respect," and "Freedom." Even the words wept with rust-stained tears that streaked the pillars.

The museum entrance, set into a redbrick wall with a stark cement walkway, featured two metal gates side by side, each with a sign above: on the left, BLANKES/WHITES, and on the right, NIE-BLANKES/NON-WHITES—a reminder of life under apartheid. We entered the museum and stepped into the painful history of our native country.

Children's drawings, photographs, writings, and posters told their stories. Black-and-white photos of known and unknown heroes, traitors, survivors, and victims hung on the stark walls. Imagined voices of the ghosts from the past told the tales of destruction and suffering. Above them all, I heard my own voice, a cry of regret for having only whispered my horror and not howled aloud my rage.

By chance of birth and luck, I was born the "right" skin color—this forecast my fate under apartheid laws, where one's racial classification determined one's status. The Nationalist government controlled the state radio; television was banned until January 1976. Certain books and writers were banned, and Blacks were required to carry passbooks. Everything was separated and segregated: schools, hospitals, buses, toilets, entrances, eating facilities, trains, living areas, even drinking fountains. At birth, every newborn was classified into one of the four race groups: Bantu (Black), Coloured (mixed-race), European (white), and Honorary White (Asian).

The Pass Act was one of the most despicable laws in the country. Blacks had to carry a passbook on them at all times, in which all their identification information was documented, including where they could live and work. Whites could come and go freely, but Blacks needed permits to move around. I remembered, as a child, watching Black men and women being arrested, handcuffed, and shoved into the backs of police vans like cattle, all for not having their passbooks with them.

In the museum, I stood quietly, my hand to my mouth, and

reflected on the photographs taken forty-five years earlier, the day of the Sharpeville massacre. The photos showed the panic and fear on the faces of the Black men, women, and children as they fled the bullets, the dead and injured bodies twisted on the ground. Their crime: peacefully protesting the passbook system. Immediately, I recalled when, as a child, I had sat on the cold cement floor listening to Nanna and watching her tears.

"I need to go outside," I said to Tom as I turned and walked toward the open doors. I put on my sunglasses and wondered if it was even possible to ever come to terms with having lived in such a violent, racist past.

Later, inside again and standing before the weapons display, I remembered the day Bob told me I had to learn to use a gun. He never told me why. But he made sure to tell me that I was a lousy shot as he grabbed my arm and told me to hold the gun steady and aim accurately. I hated the experience and refused to go back. And I've never touched a gun since that day.

A variety of weapons used during apartheid are now in the museum in a metal cage and out of reach: homemade and sophisticated, stolen and purchased, legal and illegal, their victims' names forgotten, and the killers' names lost to history. Black Africans weren't allowed to possess firearms, and the penalty for doing so was a minimum of five years in prison or even the death penalty.

Tom and I sat on a wooden bench with peeling green paint and the words EUROPEANS ONLY in big, bold, white capital letters painted on the backrest. If a Black man had sat on this bench during apartheid, he could have been jailed for up to three years or whipped ten lashes.

Tom leaned back. "It's unbelievable to think we'd see this day, sitting in the sun at an apartheid museum. As Mandela once said, 'Apartheid is where it belongs: in a museum.'"

～

Several days later, the final payment went through for our vehicle, and we set off to pick it up. We had decided on a Land Cruiser because it was the vehicle of choice for the United Nations, aid agencies, and NGOs (nongovernmental organizations, such as Oxfam) in Africa, which made it more likely that we'd be able to get spare parts. We arrived at the facility, and bubbles of excitement whirled in my stomach as we walked into the large shed. There she was, in all her mechanical, liberating beauty, her doors open as if waiting for me. For the first time, I fell in love with a vehicle.

We walked around the white Cruiser. The brown canvas rooftop tent bolted onto the roof rack would be our home for the next several months. We also carried a small tent that we could pitch on the ground. An auxiliary fuel tank allowed us to travel over a thousand miles without refueling.

An easy joy came over me. "Tom," I said, "you can come along for the ride."

This was not our first off-road vehicle. When Tom worked in exploration in southern Africa, we had lived in the bush and owned a Land Cruiser. We had learned off-road driving skills and how to use vehicle-recovery equipment—such as the high-lift jack, winch, sand ladders, and snatch towropes—the hard way. I was under no illusions regarding the challenges and possible perils we might face: driving across rivers, across the vast expanse of the Sahara Desert (almost as large as the USA), mechanical breakdowns, punctures, accidents, access to clean fuel, even the ability to right our vehicle on our own should it roll. With growing excitement, we climbed into the front seats of our new vehicle. Dials, switches, and outlets were everywhere. The Cruiser was ready, and so was I. But Tom insisted that he drive it back to Jenny and Bruce's place.

Yes, I thought, not even worrying about his executive decision. *Perhaps he's feeling excited about the trip. But will our relationship survive this journey?*

By first light, we were up and ready to leave Johannesburg and head south for Cape Town. We tossed a coin to see who would be the first to drive. After winning, I turned the ignition on, and the roar of the engine coming to life filled me with excited anticipation. I put the Cruiser into gear and pushed the accelerator, full of confidence—until the anti-hijacking alarm went off. With lights flashing and the horn blaring, the engine spluttered, and the Cruiser slowed to a crawl. While I understood that installing anti-hijacking devices in vehicles in South Africa was mandatory because of the high rate of hijackings, I cursed the device now.

Tom leaned over to the demobilizing switch but was unable to reach it. "Push the anti-hijack switch—find it quickly, before the car's immobilized."

After frantically pushing every switch I could find, the horn silenced, and the lights stopped flashing. We had covered two hundred meters, and it had taken us fifteen minutes.

It's going to be a long drive to Cairo, I thought.

The road from Johannesburg to Cape Town was eight hundred miles and passed through the Karoo, also known as the Land of Great Thirst, a vast expansive semidesert with an occasional hill. Creaking wind pumps dotted the parched landscape, their silver blades turning as they pumped water into small cement and stone farm dams. Whirlwind dust devils and tumbleweeds blew across the rocky ground. Clouds hung teasingly in the sky. We drove over the Overberg mountain range and dropped down into a lush green valley of rolling vineyards; delicate, colorful fynbos plants; and quaint cape homesteads. Soon, Cape Town appeared on the horizon.

Our first stop in Cape Town was the 4x4 Safari World Store, as we needed a satellite phone for emergency calls, a short-wave radio, and every mechanical tool Tom could think of. He asked the young salesman what he had for security. The salesman pointed to an unfamiliar, gun-like weapon. "This is the best. If someone attacks you, you shoot them, and huge flames shoot out." He flung his arm out to demonstrate the flame's path.

"Horrified," I said, "I don't want to hurt anybody. Just frighten them."

In the end, we settled for a Taser, an extendable security baton, and some Mace. But nobody would sell us a mobile phone or SIM card. To purchase these, we needed a South African identity number and a local address. As foreigners, we could buy weapons but not cell phones.

"It's illegal to sell a foreigner a phone. You can't buy one," the round, red-faced salesman said at the first phone store we entered.

At the fifth phone store, I asked the scrawny salesman behind the counter, "Tell me. Why do they need all that information from the customer?"

"Cause if you murder someone," he explained in earnest, "it'll be easier to trace you."

I shouldn't have been surprised. In 2005, South Africa did have one of the highest murder rates in the world.

"If I promise not to murder anyone, will you put a phone in your name for me?"

"Sure," he said. And we had a deal.

Tom and I agreed that we both needed to be competent in all aspects of our travels; that way, if either of us became incapacitated, the other would know enough to get us out of any situation. At the top of our training list, especially for me, was the need to refresh and upgrade our 4x4 driving and vehicle-recovery skills and knowledge. Pieter introduced himself as our instructor on our first day of training at an off-road training center outside Cape Town. Sunburned, with bleached-blond hair and a young face already weathered by the unforgiving African sun, he raised his eyebrows when I told him, "We're driving to Cairo."

Pieter explained that we would learn advanced driving skills and the limits of our heavy vehicle under extreme conditions, such as the maximum angle our loaded vehicle could negotiate a slope without rolling over. He reminded us that seat belts had to be worn—except when crossing water. At those times, the windows had to be rolled down for a quick escape if necessary. This reminded me that either Tom or I had to walk across a river to determine how deep it was before we drove across it.

"We'll toss a coin to see who gets to walk," said Tom.

Thinking about the possibility of hungry crocodiles and irritable hippos, I shook my head and said, "Oh no. Not a chance. You're a stronger swimmer than me; I'll drive. You'll walk." I was more afraid of crocodiles and hippos than the snakes or the worms that lurked in the water spreading "snail fever" (also known as bilharzia or schistosomiasis). When we lived in South Africa, Tom contracted bilharzia when he walked across a river to test the depth before we crossed it in our truck.

Pieter pointed to a picture on a board. "I'm going to review vehicle recovery, the techniques used to right your vehicle on your own should it roll or get stuck. Then we'll go drive."

Having never done any extreme off-roading or vehicle recovery without Tom, I exhaled hard, knowing how much I had to learn to be independent. But I was ready to do whatever it would take.

I approached the first extremely steep incline, which to me seemed far too steep for any vehicle. Pieter slipped into the passenger seat beside me. "Pull the seat as far forward as possible and trust your vehicle. All you'll see is sky," he said.

Glancing up at the sky, I pulled the seat forward.

"And ensure the Cruiser is in low range and the freewheeling hubs and differentials are locked."

I straightened the car to face the hill, put it into first gear, took my foot off the brake and clutch, and slowly accelerated.

"Tilt your foot onto the accelerator," Pieter said. "Give gas gently. Trust your Cruiser. Let it do its work."

I began the ascent, my hands gripping the steering wheel. He was right: all I could see was the blue, empty sky. When I reached the top, I felt ready for anything. But going down, I was convinced the car was going to tip over. As I reached the bottom, I sighed with relief and thought, *I will be able to do this without Tom at my side.*

But by the end of the day, my confidence was rattled. I struggled with the soft sand, the deep, sticky black mud, the handling of the winch and hi-lift jack, and the river crossing.

The following day, I returned to practice. I positioned the Cruiser to drive down the steep slope. "Okay, I'm ready." Then I hesitated as I looked down the precipitous incline to the muddy riverbed below. Nagging doubt crept into my belly. I didn't move. "We're going to roll."

"You'll be fine," Tom said. "Now go."

I looked around for another route down.

"Go!" he exclaimed.

Frustrated with his impatience and lack of understanding of my concerns, I glared at the steep slope and then at him. "Shut up!" I lifted my foot off the brake and lurched backward, then forward toward the steering wheel. The seat belt grabbed me as we plunged down the slope into the riverbed below.

"See, that was easy," he said. Irritated by his condescending attitude, I didn't respond. Instead, I headed over to the soft-sand course.

"You'll get bogged down if you go too slow. Keep the speed up," Tom said.

"The sand's too deep." I struggled to control the vehicle. "I'm going to get stuck."

He grabbed the steering wheel. The wheels kicked up sand; we stalled and bogged down. "You didn't listen. Now we're stuck!"

Overwhelmed by all that could go wrong and how challenging the driving was, I let go of the steering wheel. "If you don't like how

I drive, you can damn well get out and walk to Cairo." He got out, slamming the door behind him.

Tom had years of off-road-driving experience. When conditions required expert 4x4 driving skills, he always drove, and I was the passenger. I got out, sat down on the soft, warm sand, and closed my eyes. I was as stuck as the Cruiser. Tom was still in charge of my life, and I was still the passenger. Nothing had changed. But with every fiber of my being, I was determined to make change happen.

Cape Agulhas, Africa's Southern Point, 2005

Our journey north to Cairo officially started at Cape Agulhas. The most southern tip of Africa, where the warm, soothing Indian Ocean currents collide with the cold, harsh Atlantic Ocean currents from Antarctica.

We stood alone on rocks cooled by the ocean sprays and watched the two coalescing oceans tangle in an epic battle. Wind beat our bodies, and the seagulls squawked at our presence. Small beach pebbles seemed to screech as they were tossed and smashed by plunging waves.

As I watched the raging oceans before us, Tom picked up a wet stone and placed it in my hand. "Here, take this with you to Cairo."

I breathed in the sea air. I wanted to try to make our marriage work, but our relationship seemed to be in as much turmoil as the pulsating ocean before us.

"Cairo or bust," I said. "Let's go."

Our greatest danger was the possibility of an accident. The driver needed to stay alert, so we switched seats every three hours, and the passenger was always the navigator. Unable to find detailed GPS maps of Africa, Tom had purchased the US Department of Defense maps from the Cold War era, digitized them, and built our navigation system.

Isolated from the noise of the world on our long days of driving north along the west coast of South Africa toward Namibia, we chatted about things we hadn't discussed in years. We reminisced, debated, argued, and shared a few laughs. I realized that different priorities had cracked our relationship, and irrelevant news and entertainment had seeped into the crevices.

We knew more about the TV celebrities back home—what they thought, what they did, and who they were—than we did about each other. These were the people we had invited into our lives, who joined us during our mealtimes, entertained us during the evenings, and even crept into our bedroom. The TV had become the third person in our marriage. We decided right there and then to serve divorce papers to the TV on our return to Canada. I thought about how much fun we used to have before responsibilities and distractions had cluttered our lives. Reestablishing meaningful connections and dialogue began when alone, and in the hours of silence, we had time for reflection.

After several days of traveling, we arrived at a national park in South Africa's only true desert, the Richtersveld, in the country's northwestern corner. We had to register at the park entrance, as they permitted only twelve high-clearance 4x4 vehicles at any one time into this pristine wilderness. The park official informed us that the previous week a deluge rainstorm, a rare occurrence, had washed out all the tracks, including the route to the campsite. The park, known for challenging and unsophisticated trails and reputed to be South Africa's most formidable wilderness area, would be my first serious off-road challenge.

After we registered, I said I would drive. My first demanding off-road driving experience and I couldn't have chosen a more wild and exotic location. I jumped into the driver's seat, full of excitement and anxiety. I put the Cruiser into 4x4 mode and thought, *This is it. Let's go.*

I drove up and over a mountain range for several hours before dropping rapidly into the valley. The sun blazed down, the summer heat almost unbearable. But the previous week's rain had created a Richtersveld rarely experienced by anyone: a miracle of tiny, colorful flowers carpeting the arid desert landscape. Following some fresh tracks down a riverbed, through deep sand, and over rocks and boulders, we arrived at the campsite on the banks of the Gariep River.

We joined six South African campers and two Nama men who lived in the park. The names of the Nama men I don't recall, mainly because I had been unable to pronounce them due to their complex musical clicks. But I do remember that they agreed to cook the catfish the other campers had caught. To me, nothing was appealing about this five-foot-long eellike creature with a flat head and barbels like whiskers sticking out over a large gaping mouth. But the Nama men cheerfully gutted and cooked the ugly fish, wasting nothing. The fishermen told me it tasted like mud, but it was worse than mud; the bitter, fishy taste clung to my tongue.

After supper, we drank the homemade wines made by the other campers and shared tales. Everyone spoke Afrikaans, although, for Tom and me, English was our native language; bilingualism (English and Afrikaans) was compulsory for schoolchildren in South Africa. As the sweet smell of tobacco mingled with the smoke from the fire, meerkats chattered, and frogs croaked in the distance. The stars hung close, but the night would be over before I finished counting them. Sipping wine, I listened to the Nama men tell us stories about their lives, families, history, and folklore.

The Nama are nomadic herders. In the 1800s, after violent confrontations, they were forced by the colonialists to flee north from southern Africa. They now live in the park as part of a community ownership with the South African government. The succulent trees in the area, which look like men with unruly mops of hair, are called "half-man." They regard the trees as ancestors who transformed while fleeing north but who still look longingly south to the land they were forced to leave. The Nama men told of the poisonous nocturnal scorpions that lurked about, which was why their wives and children didn't live with them but instead stayed in the nearby villages. A highly poisonous puff adder snake had recently bitten one of the Nama men, but his life was saved by putting gasoline on the bite wound. They told of the rains that fell the week before and how the deluge washed out everything they owned, even their shelter. They had huddled, terrified, behind the rocks, watching a raging river created by the water coming down the side of the mountain with so much force that it rushed across the Gariep River, stopping its flow and damming it up. Never in all their lives had they seen such a thing.

I wiggled my toes in the warm sand and hugged my knees as I listened to the Nama men. I learned how they escaped the floods, fled the poisonous snakes, killed the lurking night scorpions, sought ancestral advice from the half-man trees, and protected and loved their wives and children. They had so little, and yet they could survive. I wanted to reach out and touch their strength, to learn how to live a simple life in this complex world.

Looking across the campsite fire at Tom, I wondered whether he wanted to live a simple life. Was he as ready as I was to give up our old ways of being in the world? If not, we would surely fall apart and go our separate ways, probably long before Cairo.

I thought about how our relationship had started, like a campfire, with a spark, but as the fire slowly burned out, our eyes grew accustomed to the dark without us even realizing just how much darkness our relationship had also taken on. But now, the time had come to not only see the truth but to begin to understand it in order to change it. The challenge felt daunting, and I still couldn't be sure whether Tom, let alone myself, was up to the task.

Chapter 6
Critical Relationship Communication

Namibia, 2005

In 1977 while on active duty in Namibia, Tom was thrown off a Land Rover and ended up under the wheels. The accident happened during the Namibian War of Independence. As we approached the South Africa–Namibia border, I wondered how Tom, although he'd never participated in any active action, felt about returning to the scene of such painful memories.

"I never thought you'd come with me to Cairo," I said. After believing and hoping I'd cross all these borders alone, I still had very mixed feelings about Tom coming along. There were still times when I wanted to be doing this adventure as a solo act.

He glanced at me and replied, "I never imagined that the next time was here, I'd be driving to Cairo."

We parked the Cruiser and walked to the Immigration and Customs office. A tall official behind the wooden counter examined my passport. "To write in the passport is illegal," he said. He glared at me as he waved it in the air. "Your passport is invalid."

He slammed my passport down on the counter. "You are denied your entry!"

I remembered that I had written our license plate number and emergency contact numbers in the back of my passport. "It's not illegal in Canada," I told him. "In Canada, it's the law." Then I added,

"So I hope you understand that I had to write that information in my passport."

He hesitated and glanced around. Then without a word, he stamped my passport.

Over the following days, Tom and I hiked the Naukluft Mountains' craggy peaks, dry riverbeds, and gorges. We climbed the soaring dunes of the Namib Desert, their various shapes persistently altered by winds. I felt that I had reached the end of the earth and that Calgary and all my routines were a lifetime away. Energized, we continued traveling north until we reached the remote and treacherous Skeleton Coast, known for its long history of shipwrecks and dying sailors. Drowning mariners who made it ashore found only desolation and death and heat and sand for graves. After traveling across the bleached salt roads of the Skeleton Coast, we turned east, headed inland, and set up camp in the wilderness, a stargazer's paradise, one of the earth's most naturally dark places.

Our small campfire crackled, and the smoke swirled into the early evening sky. We waited for the moon, Jupiter, the Southern Cross, and the Milky Way to light up the night sky. Suddenly, a tree branch snapped behind me, and I turned to see a gray desert elephant amble past so close that I could see his long eyelashes.

I stood up slowly and crept forward to get as near to the large animal as I dared. Tom followed behind. Adrenaline screamed through my body; the hairs on my arms stood up. All my senses sprang back to life. "Desert elephants have longer legs than other elephants," I whispered, my voice low so as not to disturb the elephant, "because they have to walk such long distances to reach water."

The tall grass rustled as the lone bull elephant walked. He stopped, and I listened as he ripped the leaves off branches with his trunk. Shrubs and branches crunched and snapped beneath his feet. His breath blew heavily. I sucked in the air, filled with the raw, sweaty smell of a wild African elephant. I glanced at Tom. His face glowed with awe. I couldn't remember the last time we had done anything so special together, so curiously intimate and moving. But the moment the elephant passed me, so close that I could have reached out and touched him, I became aware of something even more profound. With or without Tom, I belonged in Africa.

We had been on the road several weeks when Tom pulled over and stopped. It was my turn to drive. Back on the road, we chatted above the noise of the Cruiser on the dusty gravel. Suddenly, a deep depression in the road loomed up; our Cruiser hit the dip, bounced high, and landed with a heavy thud. I clutched the steering wheel hard as our vehicle swerved furiously across the road, and then I heard a new noise: *cluck-smack, cluck-smack*. I braked, slowing to a stop.

Tom got out. I heard his cry. "Shit! We've had two blowouts. Both back wheels are flat."

He unpacked the hi-lift jack and tools and then unbolted the two spare tires so he could change the flats. My hands shook as I watched him, knowing that the Cruiser could easily have rolled and possibly crushed us. A blue pickup in the distance, chased by a cloud of dust, headed our way as I focused on it to calm my panicked thoughts.

Shortly the driver stopped and leaned out his window. "What happened?" he asked.

Tom wiped his brow as he looked up. "Just had two blowouts."

The driver shrugged. "This is Africa. Shit happens."

We watched in silence as the man drove off and disappeared over the horizon, the cloud of dust continuing to follow him.

Tired and sweaty, Tom worried we wouldn't reach our destination before dark—we still had about sixty miles to go. He told me he would drive.

He got into the car and slammed the door shut. "You were going too damn fast for the road conditions."

I rolled up the window to keep out the dust. A trapped fly buzzed against my window. I reached out and crushed it, and a splattered mess smeared down the glass. I wiped my hand clean on my grubby pants and stared out the window, past the splattered fly. Trapped in my pulsating thoughts, I let the silence wash between us. The miles passed.

Then I turned to Tom and said, "The Cruiser's too damn heavy. That's why we had a blowout. I told you we're overloaded. You're taking too much stuff."

"It's not all my stuff; it's—" The Cruiser began to sway violently across the road again. "Oh shit," Tom said, trying to regain control of the car, which weaved back and forth. My seatbelt snapped hard against my chest. Stones and dust blew up.

I heard the now-familiar sound, *cluck-smack, cluck-smack*, of a flat tire on the wheel rim, a sound that we would get to know only too well. By the end of our trip, we'd rack up fourteen punctures.

Tom stopped and got out. I waited inside. Then his angry voice pierced the stillness again. "Another damn flat, this time in the front."

Because we didn't have a third spare tire, Tom repaired the flat as best he could. He stopped several times to pump the leaking tire with our portable compressor as we limped to the nearest village.

Perhaps Tom is right, I thought. *Maybe I was going too fast.* It had been a problem all my life; I'd always been rushing to meet deadlines—juggling appointments, scheduling meetings, and attending events. We had both rushed through life, and at times we could hardly keep up with each other. But I didn't want Cairo to be the destination on this trip; I wanted every moment to be an arrival.

The moon hung low in the sky when we finally arrived in the village. We set up camp, planning to get the tires repaired in the morning. Later that evening, Tom told me with conviction that he needed everything he had packed.

"We're not leaving the planet," I said. "We can always buy something if necessary." Whereas Tom was always reluctant to throw stuff out, I tended to throw out whatever I thought we'd never need or use again.

"What if we can't find what we want?" he asked.

"We'll do what we did thirty years ago when we lived in the bush. We'll improvise or find a solution." I wanted to live simply and keep only the essentials.

We negotiated: He kept his extra maps, and I kept my books. Then we tossed out every nonessential item: clothing, food, tools, and spare car parts we hoped we wouldn't need. We offered it all to curious children watching us. They gladly accepted. Nothing goes to waste in Africa.

The following day, after our tires were repaired, we headed to Etosha National Park. *This is what I live for,* I thought, *what I've been missing for too long: wilderness and wildlife.*

In the early summer evening, with the day cooling, animals congregated around the water holes in the game park. I heard the haunting, high-pitched call of the fish eagle and the plaintive whistle of the red-necked nightjar. The familiar smell of the small greenish-yellow flowers of the sweet potato that opens as the sun sets filled the air. I watched elephants quench their thirst; with no threat of predators, they lingered at the water's edge, spraying water over their backs. The rhinos moved on when the elephants appeared. Lions waited for the rhinos and elephants to finish drinking and leave before they settled in for a drink. The predators' prey—buck, giraffes, zebras, wildebeests, warthogs, kudu, jackals, and ostriches—approached the water holes tentatively, alerted to the possible danger of a predator—lion, cheetah, or leopard—lying in wait. The largest member of a herd went first. He slowly scouted the area, took a wide berth around the water hole, and only after he had approached the water to drink did the rest of the herd join him. Even then, some always remained on the lookout. Once all the animals had quenched their thirst, they quickly left the water hole—a source of life and the risk of death: water—the fatal attraction.

We always wanted to find the best campsite, a spot with shade and as level as possible so that Tom and I wouldn't roll into each other at night in our tent. When we thought we'd found the perfect spot, one of us would get out and guide the driver into the site to ensure there was nothing in the way, no low-hanging wires or branches, rocks, power outlets, or taps.

On this night, I drove into the campground. Tom waved his arm, indicating to me to come forward. I gave the Cruiser the gas, and it struggled up, seeming to be more in the air than on the ground. *Must be rocks*, I thought. I put the Cruiser into low range and gunned the engine to get over the obstacle. Tom screamed, so I took my foot off the gas pedal. He wrapped his arms around his shaking head—definitely not a good sign. I began to reverse, and Tom threw his arms up. His screeching "Noooo!" reverberated across the campground as our Cruiser bounced off the cement barrier built to protect the water tap from elephants. A fountain of water gushed up several feet into the air. The spout and pipe lay on the ground in a rapidly enlarging pool of water.

Tom ran toward me, his face red with rage. "What the hell are you doing?"

"You waved your arm to come, so I did."

He placed his big toe into the outlet, hoping to stem the flow of water.

"I wasn't telling you to come. I was pointing at another campsite."

"How the hell was I supposed to know that? It looked like you waved at me to come."

"Didn't you see the damn cement barrier?"

"Don't be stupid. Do you think I'd have driven onto it if I'd seen it?"

He repositioned his toe over the hole, and the gushing water reduced to a small fountain.

"Go get help. I'll keep my toe in the hole," he said.

I rushed off and returned with the maintenance man, but by then,

Tom had managed to screw the pipe, tap back into the outlet, and stop the water flow. We set up camp, no longer on speaking terms, but at least we had a campsite with a waterfront view.

After our supper and back on speaking terms, we agreed to be more diligent with our hand signals when directing the driver. We also needed to be precise and stay present in the moment when talking to each other. Clear communication was critical; a mistake could cost us our lives. Like many couples, Tom and I made too-frequent use of "I told you so," "You never listen to me," and "I never said that"; indeed, they'd become part of our daily chatter. I told Tom he talked too much, his message lost in the garble. He countered that I didn't say enough and hated my silence. In general, we didn't always listen; we made assumptions, never clarified, or, at worst, ignored each other completely.

But over time, our communication skills slowly improved. We learned to communicate with signs and nods and in code. We introduced our twenty-minute rule: if we disagreed, we had twenty minutes to sulk, and then we had to pull together again. We never knew what was waiting for us around the next bend. I began to realize that our relationship had no absolutes; it was all a dance, never static. Just as situations regularly changed, so did our relationship.

After three weeks of traveling through Namibia, it was time to leave. As I stood on the banks of the Kunene River and watched the hippos laze in the water, I bid farewell to Namibia. I wondered what surprises lay ahead as we crossed into Botswana.

Botswana, 2005

The Okavango River, known as "the river that never finds the ocean," flows into Botswana, spreading out into an inland delta and then disappearing down into a crack in the earth beneath the sands of the Kalahari Desert. The Okavango Delta, to my immense delight, is an oasis teeming with wildlife.

A campsite on the outskirts of Maun, the gateway to the Okavango Delta and the Moremi Game Reserve and Chobe National Park, served as our base while we explored Botswana. In the dark of one night, I heard drums and singing in the distance. A high wire fence surrounded the campsite, and the gate was locked. I wasn't sure if the locked gate was to keep the campers in or the wildlife out, although I speculated it was to keep campers from coming in to stay free for the night.

I asked Tom if he wanted to join me (I was prepared to go alone) and head off in the direction of the music. When we couldn't find the guard to open the gate, we climbed over the fence, dropped to the ground, and headed off across the veld. The beams of our flashlights penetrated the blackness, and I heard the rustle of life around us as we walked toward the music. The experience was quite unnerving, but it felt good to be back in the bush with adrenaline racing through my body.

Fifteen minutes later, we arrived at a fire smoldering alongside a reed enclosure. Behind the reeds, the sounds of rhythmic drumbeats, shuffling feet, clapping hands, and melodic voices filled the warm night air. As we tentatively approached the enclosure, a man came out and greeted us in English. I asked if we could please join in. He ushered us inside the enclosure, situated beneath a large acacia tree. Its branches and the starry night sky formed the roof, reeds the walls, and the bare earth formed the floor. I joined the women and children while Tom joined the men.

A pole stood in the center, alongside glowing embers and ash placed in a shovel. Candles stuck in the dirt emitted a faint light. Babies slept on threadbare pieces of cloth on the ground; barefooted children giggled at our arrival, and adults swayed to the beat. Behind a small wooden pulpit stood a middle-aged man gowned in white. He welcomed us to their church. Then the entire congregation welcomed us in English and said how pleased they were to have us join. "We never before had anyone of your kind join us in prayer," they said.

I didn't understand a word of the service conducted in Setswana, one of the main languages of Botswana. Yet I stood transfixed, the air electric. I immediately thought of my childhood and especially of Nanna. She would don her Sunday dress each Sunday, but I never asked her about her church or where she went to pray. *Did she, too, pray under a tree?* I now wondered.

Two women, each with an infant strapped onto her back, and two men sat in the front. The pastor blessed them and sprinkled water and ashes over their heads. Swaying to the beat of the drums, singing, and clapping, we all rhythmically shuffled around the smoldering embers, the air filled with smells of smoke and sweat. Women paused to sprinkle water over the smoldering fire and held their bare feet above the ashes. Finally, the pastor thanked us for attending and asked us to say something. After I expressed our gratitude for being so warmly welcomed, an elderly gray-haired man apologized for their "poor church." He went on, "It's our church. It is not much because we live in poverty, but now we have our meal and would like you to stay and eat with us."

They shared their fried roll of dough and warm water with us. The pastor sprinkled water and ash over Tom and me as he blessed us. The evening ended. It had been over two hours since our arrival, and we left amid the cheers of warm farewells.

Humbled by the experience and touched by the generosity of the people, I walked quietly alongside Tom, his bare arms brushing against mine. The high-pitched, shrill buzz of the cicada beetles and other night critters filled the air. I felt welcomed back home to Africa, and my faith in humanity felt renewed.

But other life-forms on earth have never lost my faith, and I was eager to explore more of what wild Africa has to offer. Because of their gentle nature and tendency to take care of one another, especially their young, elephants are my favorite wild animal, and I wanted to be close to them again. I stood on the banks of the Chobe and watched the tourists' boats cruise down the center of the wide brown river.

But I longed for a small boat that would take us closer to the banks. Louwrens, a local, introduced us to Allen, a young, energetic man. He wore shorts, no shirt, and no shoes, his black hair wild and curly. His brown eyes smiled with mischief, and he didn't look a day over twenty.

"Allen grew up on the Chobe River, and nobody can get as close to the wildlife as he can," Louwrens explained.

After our best efforts at cajoling and pleading, Allen agreed to take us out onto the river in his little boat, with an outboard engine at the rear. Allen got on board and offered safety instructions as we stood on the riverbank.

"Hippos are our biggest threat. If they attack the boat, swim down and then as far away as you can from the boat." The little engine spluttered to life. "You must dive deep, so we don't wear life jackets."

I hesitated, not sure what to do. I glanced across the river and saw the hippos. "Swimming away from an enraged hippo in a crocodile-infested river is not my idea of safety," I said.

Tom turned to me and countered, "You're the one that keeps telling me you are willing to risk it all."

He was right: I had said that. But now I wondered just how much I was prepared to risk; I also wondered if Tom would follow me into the small boat.

"Hurry up, we needed to leave," said Allen.

I looked back out across the river, not seeing any crocodiles. *This is it*, I thought, and I climbed into the little boat. Tom followed.

Humungous hippopotamuses watched us pass by and sank below the water when we came too close. Crocodiles drifted lazily past. Allen went far up the river, away from the tourist boats, as engine noises disturb the wildlife. After an hour, we saw a large herd of elephants ambling down the steep bank toward the river. Allen cut the engine, and we drifted toward the shore. The great matriarch led the herd to the bank. A tiny newborn with its umbilical cord still attached, perhaps only a few hours old, followed closely behind. The elephants drank and, with their trunks, sprayed cool water over their bodies. The baby stood hesitantly on the bank, then slipped and fell into the river. I held my breath as he struggled forever before his tiny trunk finally rose above the water. He waved it around as if not quite sure what to do with it. The older matriarch of the herd watched closely, protecting and helping the baby with her trunk and feet. When the young mother finished drinking, she walked toward her newborn. He struggled to his feet and nudged her nipples, searching for milk. Once the infant was with its mother, only then did the older matriarch take her turn to drink.

The evening before we moved on, I asked Tom what the highlight had been for him in Botswana. He recalled an evening in Moremi Game Reserve: "The night the lions were prowling near our Cruiser when you were on top in the tent, too scared to go down?"

The basic campsite was unfenced to maintain the wilderness experience. At night, I'd been concerned, hearing hippos rumble and the roar of lions in the distance. I'd scanned the trees with my flash-light, looking for the glint of leopard eyes. Our tent canvas offered no protection, and I'd hoped the lions were too lazy to climb up onto the roof of our Cruiser. I certainly knew a leopard would climb up if tempted; leopards are skilled tree climbers. I could think of nothing else except our vulnerability to attack. But more than anything, my thoughts of danger made me feel alive again. Paradoxically, even a sense of peace began to tap me on my shoulder. And one other point became crystal clear: Tom and I both shared a love of the African wilderness and wildlife.

We planned to cross into Zimbabwe the following morning, so we packed up everything except what we'd need for breakfast. As the sun dipped into the Chobe River, we set off for an evening stroll. Hippos bellowed, and willow trees cast long shadows over the brown flow-ing water. I listened to the call of a male red-chested cuckoo, "*weet, weet, weeo*," and then the shrilled response, "*pipipipi*," of his partner.

This back-and-forth is one of the most familiar birdcalls in Southern Africa and was my favorite bird sound as a child.

We reminisced about the time we visited Zimbabwe in 1970, then still known as Rhodesia. We had headed there to see the newly built Kariba Dam on the Zambezi River, which created the world's largest man-made lake. During the building of the dam wall, the newly formed lake behind it flooded the valley for 143 miles. Lake Kariba became the scene of Operation Noah, one of the most miraculous wilderness-rescue efforts in history.

Between 1958 and 1962, Rupert Fothergill headed a group of eleven fearless, wildly spirited men who fought against time and impossible odds with rudimentary equipment and their ingenuity to rescue wildlife trapped on islands in the rising waters. Operation Noah, a fight against a wildlife catastrophe, is still the world's largest animal-rescue mission. In hippo- and crocodile-infested waters, the men rescued fear-crazed rhinos; herded drowning, exhausted elephants and lions; snared poisonous snakes clinging to life in treetops; trapped, carried, darted, and roped over six thousand animals—warthogs, monkeys, buffalo, buck, anteaters, porcupines, leopards, and more—bringing them to safety on the mainland. During our visit to Lake Kariba in 1970, we met some of the men involved in Operation Noah. There I first learned of the real threat to wildlife: the human desire for material progress that willingly sacrifices all species in its path. Rupert Fothergill died in 1975 and was one of Africa's greatest wildlife rangers and advocates.

The building of the Kariba Dam also resulted in the worst resettlement disaster in Africa. The displacement of the Tonga people resulted in fifty-seven thousand "development refugees." The despair and anger of the Tonga people still hung in the air over the valley.

That night I lay in bed, believing we would be heading back to Zimbabwe in the morning. Little did we know that our plans would not work out as expected.

Chapter 7
Romance Is Dangerous

The Zimbabwean newspaper headline read PROSTITUTES DEMAND PAYMENT IN DIESEL—not an enticing invitation to a country. Under the dictatorship of President Mugabe, Zimbabwe had been plunged into guerrilla warfare. So, given the shortage of everything—including fuel—we decided not to go to Zimbabwe. Tom had worked in Zimbabwe before we left South Africa, and we wanted to revisit Victoria Falls and Lake Kariba. One can see the falls from Zambia, but in Zimbabwe, the falls embrace you with their roar and spray of mist. However, a visit to Zimbabwe without guaranteed access to fuel just wasn't feasible.

Zambia, 2005
We drove onto the Kazungula Ferry and parked on its deck straddling blue pontoons, and we crossed the Zambezi River into Zambia. Coming from orderly Botswana, we were jolted into the Zambian hustle as we disembarked. A tall man, neatly dressed in a blue shirt and jeans, sunglasses elegantly placed on his shaved head, approached Tom and asked if he "wanted to change money." He introduced himself as Kim, an official. Voluble but polite, Kim turned out to be our first encounter with a scam artist, and he taught us a valuable lesson. It cost us $10, but once we realized he'd scammed us, we honed the skills needed to negotiate with money changers, men quick with their hands and words, and never again did we fall for a money-changing scam.

From then on, we always negotiated a better deal with the money changers in the local markets and back alleys than we could with any banks or foreign exchanges. And eventually, as a couple, were able to outwit all scam artists.

Despite having a solar panel, maintaining enough power for our electronic equipment was a constant challenge. So, when we had access to an outdoor electrical power outlet at the campsite at Livingstone, we thought we'd hit pay dirt. Despite the bolts of lightning flashing across the night sky and the rain beating down, Tom crept around in the storm. Like a frenzied electrician, he fussed with the electrical extension cord, power bar, and adapters. He plugged in cameras, flashlights, computers, auxiliary batteries, and our satellite phone and cell phone to recharge. He inserted the final plug into the electrical socket, and immediately the campsite was plunged into impenetrable blackness.

Tom snuck back into the car. "I think I just did that. I've tripped the damn campsite fuses." We waited for the power to be restored. Time passed. The rain continued to beat down, and lightning streaked across the heavens. A man holding a large plastic bag over his head hurried by, and Tom rolled down the window. "Do you know when they will get the power back?" he asked. Without stopping, the man informed us, "Big, big problem. Everybody in the town. No power anywhere."

"Dammit," said Tom as he got out of the car to remove all evidence of what he had just done.

The following morning, we wandered around central Livingstone and chatted with a friendly shop owner. He told us about the "terrible storm" and how "the lightning hit the power transformer." Our assumptions had been wrong, as so many of my assumptions about the world, myself, and Tom proved incorrect. Sometimes I was embarrassed by how little I knew or how wrong I was. What gave birth to my ill-informed opinions and beliefs about the world, about Tom, and even about myself?

At home, I rarely even had to think about access to electricity or clean water. But life was not so straightforward in some parts of the world.

The following day, en route to the city of Lusaka, we set up camp in the bush. It was dusk; the sycamore fig trees sprinkled shadows across the grass. Cheeky, red-faced mousebirds whistled, "*chi vu vu, chi vu vu*," as they returned home to rest in the acacia thorn trees and scrub around us. Tom started a small fire and began to cook while I searched for more dry logs and kindling, smacking my arms and legs when the mosquitoes attacked as they did every day at dusk. I began to think that a mixture of sweat, DEET, and sunscreen was a highly valued delicacy for mosquitoes, insects who left an itchy calling card at best, or, at worst, malaria. The tiny, quiet, malaria-carrying mosquitoes are from the *Anopheles* genus. With them, there is no loud, whining siren, no large flying object headed for you. They attack in silence and move on, their stomachs bloated. The Cruiser's windows were already a maze of my handprints and splats of my blood, a sign of the desperate daily war between the formidable insects and me. I had become a mosquito fast-food fly-through, and our camper lights the flashing neon sign advertising my blood type, which they seemed to prefer to Tom's.

By the time Tom called me for supper, the sun had sunk below the horizon. I walked over and looked at the steak sizzling atop the glowing coals. I paused, puzzled. "Why is the meat moving?" Reaching for a flashlight to closely examine the squirming meat, I saw, to my amazement, that our dinner was alive with bugs. Our camp light attracted the nocturnal insects of the world, and our supper had become theirs. The tiny bugs attracted the bigger bugs, which attracted the even-larger ones. I watched in mortified silence.

Tom picked up the meat, said, "Only one solution," and, with a swipe of his knife, knocked most of the insects onto the ground. "If there're any left," he said, "they're cooked." So began my adaptation to surviving with few options or choices.

From Lusaka, the capital of Zambia, to the South Luangwa National Park, the road passes through one village after another, but I felt no sense of monotony. Vendor stalls and goods spilled over onto the roadside, with freshly baked bread, fish and tomatoes, bags of charcoal, straw baskets and mats, wooden curios and bowls, fake gems, beds, and secondhand dresses, pants, shoes, and shirts for sale. English is the country's official language, but many rural villagers speak little or no English. All children, however, knew two English sentences: "I am an AIDS orphan" and "I need money for schoolbooks." Unfortunately, our handing out of free school supplies resulted in fights between the bigger children and the little ones, so we abandoned the idea of giving out gifts altogether. Giving is complicated and has many unintended consequences.

After several days of travel, we arrived at the South Luangwa preserve, one of Africa's largest wildlife sanctuaries. At the Flatdogs camp, the park ranger informed us that "hippos pass through the camp about nine in the evening. The elephants between five and six in the morning, and they will smash car windows to get to food. Also, hyenas wander the campgrounds at night. So be very, very careful."

Heeding his warning, I took our food and locked it up in the elephant-proof container, noticing as I did the wooden platforms high up in the trees where campers pitched their small tents.

Tom, true to his nature, insisted that the arrangement was romantic. "We can pitch our pup tent on a platform."

I reluctantly agreed to his suggestion, knowing we would be out of reach of wandering hippos, ambling elephants, and scavenging hyenas. I even thought it might be fun.

It was already eight thirty when he called down to me from the tree. "It's all ready. I've even got us candles and some wine."

The hippos will arrive soon, I thought, as I climbed the creaky wood-and-rope ladder to the small wooden platform, twenty feet in the air with no railing. "You've got to be kidding," I said upon arrival.

Our small tent was bigger than the platform, so the tent edges hung over the side. "There's no way I'm sleeping up here. It's not safe."

"I wondered about that," replied Tom. "But if we put something at the tent door to remind us not to step out, we'll be fine."

"You're crazy. I'm not sleeping up here." I began to climb back down.

Tom blew out the candles. "I'll take this tent down tomorrow. We need to get our rooftop tent up before the hippos arrive." He followed me down, and our romantic evening died.

Tom was always the more romantic one in our relationship. My pragmatism stalled me on most of my attempts. Not for the first time, but perhaps with more clarity, I realized just how different Tom and I were from each other. I had always told him, "Romance is dangerous. It seduces one down a path that one may later regret" (like falling off a platform into the path of a hippo). In my mind, romance creates a false warm glow, an ephemeral illusion of intimacy. Yet Tom, knowing how I felt, continued to buy me flowers and cards. Then again, perhaps without some version of meaningful romance, other vital connections won't survive. In our relationship, intimacy had all but disappeared, and I had no idea how or whether we could reclaim it. But I did know reclaiming it wasn't going to happen on that rickety platform in a large deciduous sausage tree.

Two days later, heading back to Chipata, Tom hit the brakes as we careered toward a sharp bend in the muddy, potholed road, but the Cruiser didn't respond. Tom applied all his force to the brakes and slammed the stick into low gear. The Cruiser shuddered to a stop. On inspection, he discovered that the brake fluid was leaking and we had no brakes. Fortunately, the backup emergency brakes had kicked in. We had no choice but to hope that the emergency brakes would hold for the challenging off-road driving still ahead.

After several tense hours, we pulled into a garage in the village of Chipata. Vehicle wrecks and used parts lined the white-painted brick wall surrounding the work compound. While Tom went to find the owner, I watched the welder yell instructions to a young man standing on a ramp next to a pole. The young man held the ends of two wires connected to the welding machine, one in each hand. He touched these to the tangled wires hanging down from the overhead electrical grid, and the welding machine spluttered into action. The welding rod arced as the welder worked. The welder yelled again, and the young man separated the two wires. The welding machine quieted. Not understanding the language, I imagined the welder shouting, "Okay, now!" and "Okay, stop!" each time he instructed the young man with the wires. This risky setup was their electrical supply.

Tom drove up onto the ramp above the work pit. On inspection, he saw the left rear brake pads had shredded, and all the brake fluid was gone. Naph, the garage owner, told us we were lucky he had new brake pads. Smiling widely, he emphasized the word "new."

Repairing the brake fluid issue was a bigger problem. Naph needed to replace the hydraulic cylinder, and he didn't have one. "No problem," he assured us. "I find used one in town; somebody has one."

Naph didn't own a jack that fitted our Cruiser, and because of limited space over the pit, we could not use our jack. The mechanics began constructing a makeshift support system to ensure our car didn't fall into the work pit. The construction was so precarious that Tom found a wheel rim from a truck and placed it under the chassis. Standing in the pit beneath the Cruiser, the mechanics began the repair. Suddenly I heard a loud crash followed by screams. I watched, horrified, as our car smashed down hard onto the truck's wheel rim. Men covered in dust, grease, and blood emerged from the pit and beneath the fallen car, holding their heads. "Eh, we nearly died," one said. They laughed and dusted themselves off before propping our car up yet again so they could return to work beneath it.

Naph left to find a cylinder, and the mechanics took a break. A middle-aged man who introduced himself as Jack joined us in the shade of the pawpaw tree along with the mechanics. Jack told us he was a teacher. He'd heard that we were at the garage and so had come to talk to us. "So I can better my English," he said.

The conversation was casual, and Jack assisted with the translations. The mechanics were curious about us. They asked, "Where you from?" "What you do?" "Where you go?" They told us they had met *muzungu*—white people—traveling before, but the "*muzungu* did not talk much" to them. Jack told us how difficult it was to find teachers, especially those with training. He paused, leaned back with his hands resting on the red soil behind him, and looked at us.

"We have it better than white people," he said, and he sat back up. "White people don't like each other. They have money. We have no money. We depend on each other; we have to help each other. We have to like each other."

His comment felt like a fist to my gut.

Jack was right. I had the option to walk away from my privileged life. But in the Cruiser, there was nowhere for either Tom or me to go, nowhere to hide, no one else to talk to, no one else to depend on. We had only each other, and we had to work out and negotiate our differences. The situation was an opportunity but still an unsettling one.

After a week, we bid farewell to our Chipata friends and mechanics and drove toward the Zambia-Malawi border. The Malawian border officials were efficient and honest. Taking a car across most borders in Africa proved to be demanding, with considerable paperwork required. Indeed, by the end of our journey, I concluded that it would be easier to smuggle people than cars across a border.

Malawi, 2005
Once in Malawi, we set out to buy supplies. At a bustling market, we parked in the shade alongside a bus that had arrived just moments before us. Bold letters across the back window spelled out "In God

We Trust." Hawkers rushed toward the bus and held up grass platters loaded with fresh mangoes, pawpaws, bananas, boiled eggs, and bottled water to the passengers, who were leaning out the open windows. Vendors shoved, pushed, and called out, and boisterous bargaining began. Around us, women with infants strapped onto their backs clutched their toddlers' hands and balanced bags on their heads as they walked. Men carrying bundles of food, wood, clothing, and even curios made their way to their stalls. Bicycle taxis loaded with goods or people weaved between pedestrians and vehicles. More people scrambled from overloaded minibus taxis and shouted above the sounds of disorder and chaos.

With increasing pleasure, I breathed in the assorted smells of raw life. Food boiled and sizzled over smoky charcoal fires, goats tied to trees bleated, chickens squawked as they awaited their fate, and scrawny brown dogs scavenged for scraps. Children played on the piles of donated scruffy shoes, which were for sale. Well-worn jeans and faded name-brand T-shirts, also for sale, fluttered in the breeze. An elderly tailor, stern yet welcoming to his customers, treadled his sewing machine in the shade of his stall. The men's suits he had sewn hung from a rack. He told us he also sold the donated clothing, which arrived in containers from "far away." We continued to see donated products for sale in markets, including expired medications, foreign-language children's books, and, once, even weight-loss products in a place where hunger is a daily challenge faced by many.

We returned to our Cruiser, and I got in to drive into Lilongwe, the capital of Malawi. In cities, whenever Tom drove and I navigated, we fought, we argued: "I said *turn*, you missed it." "That's *not* a road!" "It *is* a road." "You give bad directions." "You need to drive better." We were like sparring partners. Yet if we switched roles and I drove in cities, we became a well-oiled driving team. Our arrangement worked, though precisely why remained a mystery.

We found the Toyota dealership in the old section of Lilongwe, which bustled with traditional life. Unfortunately, the dealership didn't have a new part for our repaired brake, so we could only hope that the secondhand Zambian brake part would last. With no need to linger in Lilongwe, Tom wanted to leave immediately.

I looked at my watch. "It's too late to leave. It's almost 5:30. We'll have to stay here for the night." By midafternoon, we always started to look for a place to camp for the night.

"No, I want to get out of here. Let's go. We'll find a place out of town."

There is no dusk in Africa. It's day, and then it's night. "What if we can't find a place before dark?"

"Come on, let's go," he argued. "We'll find somewhere."

Against my better judgment and instincts, I decided to go along with Tom's developing sense of confidence. But as we left, I felt an uneasiness about the approaching African night that I hadn't noticed before. The land is warm and welcoming, but if common sense is sacrificed for adventure in remote locations, Africa can be a very unforgiving continent.

Darkness settled around us quickly. There were no streetlights, many vehicles had no working headlights, and no one seemed to have brake lights. People, cows, goats, and donkeys wandered into the road.

I sensed an accident waiting to happen. "Tom, we need to stop driving," I said urgently. "You're right." But it was too dark for us to find a safe place to camp.

Suddenly our Cruiser lurched up and bounced over something. "What the hell was that?" said Tom, slamming on the brakes. In the darkness, we couldn't see anything. Tom got out and walked around to the front of the car.

A human form struggling to sit up growled at Tom. "You no see me. I put stick there."

I got out and saw Tom had run over a log placed on the road. Fortunately, he was going slow and had braked in time so that he hadn't run over the man sleeping behind the log, the man's protective barrier.

"Why are you sleeping on the road?" Tom snapped. "It's dangerous."

The swaying man stood up. "It's warm; it's good."

Tom grabbed the log from under the Cruiser, pulled it out, and tossed it onto the side of the road. "Bloody stupid man," he muttered as we returned to the Cruiser. "I'll pull in as soon I see a place we can stay," he added.

At the next village, we stopped at a little pink shack with a sign that read GUEST HOUSE. A few hours later, as we lay on the worn mattress beneath a gray threadbare mosquito net in the guest house, Tom agreed to never again drive at night. Even so, the nights would bring their fair share of surprises.

Chapter 8
Alone in the World

Malawi, 2005
Several days later, we set up camp on the sandy shores of Lake Malawi near a sign that read:

WARNING
HIPPOS HAVE BEEN KNOWN TO COME ONTO THE
BEACHES AFTER 5.00 PM.
WE RECOMMEND YOU DO NOT WALK ON THE BEACHES
OR SWIM DURING THE HOURS OF DARKNESS.

Black clouds of lake flies hovered in the midday sky. Fishermen in wooden dugouts flung their red nets into the lake, which has the largest number of fish species (estimated to be between seven hundred and one thousand species of cichlids) in the world. The lake supplies the livelihood for most people; they rely on it for water, irrigation, food, fishing, recreation, and transportation. The 650-tonne ferry *MV Ilala* travels the length of the lake weekly, hauling goods and people, and is the lifeline for communities along the way. Some locals call Lake Malawi the "calendar lake," as it is fifty-two miles wide and an astonishing 350 miles long.

That evening, I sat near the beach and watched the sun disappear into the lake. Lights from the fishing dugouts twinkled like stars in the distance. The scene was peaceful until Tom suddenly emerged from the water as a wild man possessed.

71

Between his panting breaths, he yelled, "I forgot about the warning sign. Fuck! I've never swum so fast in my life." He gulped the air. "I thought I was a dead man." His chest heaved as he spoke, and he waved his arms over his head as if he were still swimming. "I am so damn hot; I just had to cool off. We've got to rethink this trip—we're crazy."

The more he spoke, the wilder he looked, his beard untamed, his eyes red with fury, his body tense. The camp owner had also warned us that crocodiles also lived in the lake.

"The heat, the bugs, what the hell are we doing here?" he continued.

He walked toward me and roughly grabbed my arms. "My body's on fire." His hands burned on my skin. "We need to go home."

I pushed his hands away. "I'm not going home. You can go. I'm going to Cairo."

Just then, two young locals emerged from the shadows, and a sweet, sweaty smell rose in the air. "Eh, you want some *chamba*— marijuana?" One stretched out his hand and offered us a joint. "Good stuff." I shook my head no. The young men laughed and returned to the shadows.

"I'm going," I said, and I turned and walked away. Then I turned around and yelled back, "You've got to drink more water. I keep telling you that."

As Tom and I lay in the tent in the sweltering heat of the night, I smacked the mosquitoes off my face. I heard my mother's voice and her solution to everything: "Drink water; that's what the lions drink." *Have I become like my mother?* With her emotions stunted, she always struggled to show compassion. *Drink more water; is that all I have to offer?* I knew Tom suffered in extreme heat.

Suddenly a loud thud, followed quickly by another, interrupted my thoughts.

Tom bolted upright. "What the hell was that?"

"It's probably falling mangoes," I muttered. "Remember," I

stressed, "you insisted on parking under the mango tree? And I told you they're in season."

I got up and walked down to the lake—the night sky filled with millions of stars. Calm waves lapped up onto the sand and around my feet. I soaked a towel and returned to our tent. I placed the dripping-wet towel over Tom. "You'll feel better when your temp's down." I offered him more water.

Since leaving Cape Town, we had laughed and shared more than we had done in the prior three years. I was optimistic we could reclaim our relationship, but I still had more work to do. I couldn't simply dismiss his concerns if I wanted him to continue this trip with me.

Tom always took his time, whereas I was impatient. "You walk too slow," I'd complain. "Keep up." Or "You read too slow." He once asked what my passion was, and I told him, "To be where I'm not." I constantly needed to be on the move. My curiosity about the world was both my strength and my weakness. I live my life fast-forward, and Tom lives his on replay. But Africa wouldn't be any kind of tonic for what ailed me if I didn't learn from the experience. On this night, I decided I needed to hit my pause button and linger while at the lake. I didn't want Tom to push the stop button and end it all. He required his time to catch up, reflect, and replay, and I had to slow down; I had to pause. We moved through the world so differently. It was no wonder that, at times, we struggled to understand each other.

The following morning, I stood on the shore, eating a sweet, warm, and juicy mango. Afterward, I recommended that we pack up and head to Cape Maclear for some scuba diving in the lake several miles offshore, away from crocodiles and hippos (a Navy diver in his younger days, Tom was still passionate about scuba). I also suggested that we plan to scuba dive off Zanzibar, swim with whale sharks off the coast of Mombasa, and celebrate our arrival in Egypt by diving in the Red Sea. He smiled and said, "Sure." On our trip, we had started learning to work together; now, we needed to learn to just be with each other—alone in the world but as equal partners.

Without question, I had to change. I needed to stop chasing that illusory dream of fierce and total independence. I no longer wanted that much isolation. I wanted to have a person in my life whom I could depend on when I was fragile or broken. And I wanted to be there for Tom when he needed support. Deep down, however, I knew that our relationship still faced many challenges. Tom would have to change, and so would I.

We bounced down the corrugated, dusty road to Cape Maclear at Lake Malawi National Park, located at the south end of the lake. At Scuba Shack, a medium-sized tail-wagging brown mutt greeted us. It seemed closely related to every dog I had met in Malawi. A young man eventually came along and introduced himself as Dulani. He was pleased to arrange a dive for us and made a quick phone call. Soon after, a little white boat powered by an outboard motor arrived. I helped load our yellow scuba tanks and other diving equipment so that we could head out to Thumbi Island.

After thirty minutes, Dulani stopped and threw a small anchor overboard. Tom and I checked each other's equipment. I put my mask on, inserted the regulator into my mouth, took a few breaths, gave the thumbs-up sign that all was well, and then rolled backward off the boat.

Fish eagles skimmed and dived into the waters around me as I entered the warm, clear water and the world's largest freshwater aquarium. Millions of curious cichlids moved between my bubbles as I swam and dived in their world. Deep blue with orange fins, a "marmalade cat" cichlid swam among the cluster of round boulders close to the island. Each blink of my eyes seemed to conjure up another vivid display. Electric-yellow fish with distinctive black stripes swam past a shoal of salmon-colored cichlids. Blue, red, and green cichlids darted among a school of shimmering white fish, which hid between the plants. Some nibbled at the algae on the rocks; others drifted down to the sand on the bottom. It was as if someone had dumped multiple cans of colored paint into the water, creating rainbows that broke apart and swam in all directions.

Afterward, Tom climbed back into the boat. "That was one of my best dives ever!" he exclaimed. His face gleamed with happiness as he reached out to help me remove my gear. He smiled and said, "You did great."

With the sun on my face and the breeze in my hair, I felt like an old friend had returned. I passed a bottle of water to Tom. "Drink up. Next dive, Zanzibar."

We made our way north along the lakeside, stopping at times to camp. We had by now developed a daily routine. At the end of the day, Tom set up camp, and I wandered into the nearest village to meet the locals. I chatted with the mothers and played with the children. I watched the men mend their nets on the beach and the boys catch little fish. The following morning when Tom went into the village or walked along the beach, the children ran up and greeted him with, "Where's Janet?"

No longer just *Tom's wife*, I had my name again. Attending staid corporate oil and gas events in Calgary, I had earned the nickname Mona Lisa, the spouse with a mysterious smile. I shared nothing, and I played my role with grace and decorum. But beneath my mask, I wanted to dance on the tables. In Africa, I began to feel that my world was becoming a table of immense riches.

Driving on corrugated roads resulted in constant vibrations, which finally caused the bolt that attached the Cruiser's outside spotlight to shear off. Convinced I could find someone in a village that could get a bolt for us, I said, "I'll get someone who'll help us."

"You're an optimist. Nobody will have a bolt the exact size we need."

I put the word out, and the following day a middle-aged man

approached Tom and introduced himself as Mr. Fixer. He had walked several miles from his home to tell us he could repair the spotlight.

We all got into the Cruiser and drove down a dusty track to his home and workshop. In a courtyard between his house and a tin shed, Mr. Fixer kept his tools, along with a workbench and vise. In the shade of three large fever trees, he set up his tools and called two men to help him handcraft a bolt.

For several hours, I watched the men's polished performances and skills. But I also thought about how Tom and I had changed on this trip and were becoming more resourceful, how our safe suburban lives in Canada had weakened our resilience and ability to be self-sufficient. I also loved reaching out to the locals and asking them for help when we needed it—asking for help constantly developed into a community event and a chance to learn about them, their families, and their lives. And I marveled at the ingenuity of the locals; they taught me so much.

While they worked, we drank sweet black tea and chatted with Mr. Fixer and his two assistants, Moses and Peter. Finally, Mr. Fixer walked up to the Cruiser and inserted the bolt, which attached the spotlight precisely, as he'd planned. He beamed with pride. "It fits perfectly." He insisted on giving Tom a receipt for payment. In a beautiful cursive script, he wrote his name, the date, "one bolt," and the payment amount on a plain piece of white paper. After a warm farewell, we packed up and continued to make our way.

In the early 1900s, the Scottish Presbyterian missionaries in Malawi regularly died of malaria, yellow fever, and other nasty bacteria and viruses that crept into their bodies. Like Tom, they, too, struggled in the heat on the shores of Lake Malawi. But their prayers were answered in 1905 when they decided to build a village at the top of the Nyika Plateau, which rises almost a mile and overlooks the lake. The air is cooler up there, and the malaria-loaded mosquitoes less bothersome. But first, the Scots had to build a road. I imagined the missionaries standing on the shores, looking up past the first few miles of the gentle slope to the steep rise of the mountain. They had to hack through the thick vegetation, chop down trees, move rocks, and cut a narrow dirt track zigzagging with twenty-two switchbacks. Actually, I imagined the sunburned white Scots standing in the shade of a large acacia tree, sipping tea, giving orders, and supervising the local men who toiled and sweated under the searing sun as they built the road for the missionaries.

I turned to Tom. "It looks too steep and narrow. Everyone says the road's too dangerous and in terrible condition and that we should take the new road up to Livingstonia."

Much like a Scottish Presbyterian missionary, Tom puffed out his chest and said, "It can be done."

"You know I loathe roads that are incredibly steep and barely wide enough for our vehicle." I hated to look down out of the passenger window and see rocks that our tires had set free, tumbling down from the crumbling edges of the road and disappearing to the valley floor hundreds of feet below.

"You can close your eyes—I'll drive. We'll be fine, sweetheart." He sounded confident.

I recalled an incident in Botswana when we were driving across a raised gravel dyke. The track on top was only as wide as the Cruiser, with sharp scree slopes down on either side. I held my breath as Tom drove. Suddenly a front wheel hit a boulder, which pushed the Cruiser to the left, leaving the left front wheel hanging precariously over the edge.

"Oh shit!" said Tom. "Quickly get out and direct me back into the track."

I opened the door, stepped into the air, and slid down the steep scree slope on my bottom.

"You didn't close the door!" Tom called out.

When I finally came to a stop, I looked up; the front passenger door hung open.

Tom was concerned that the open door would add to the problem of maintaining stability.

"You need to come back and close the door. Quickly. Before the vehicle rolls."

I struggled on my hands and knees to climb back up the steep scree slope. Reaching the top, I gently pushed the bottom of the door and closed it. For a moment, I'd wondered, *Will the Cruiser come tumbling down and crush me?*

With real reluctance and against my better judgment, I agreed to let Tom drive up the narrow, winding, nine-mile gravel track to Livingstonia, a small village on the top of the plateau. Could I trust him? It's always a fine line between trust and distrust, even between long-married couples.

"You'll be fine, sweetheart," Tom said as we set off.

The journey took two hours, as most of the twenty-two switchbacks required careful three-point turns to navigate the corners. Gingerly hugging the edge of the mountain, with a sheer drop hundreds of feet down on one side, Tom drove cautiously up. The view is said to be the most spectacular in Malawi, but I can't confirm this since I never took my eyes off the track. At the same time, I used my best backseat driver skills to help Tom: "Be careful." "Watch the edge." "Don't hit that rock!" And just like a missionary, I prayed.

Tom continued to reassure me: "You're fine, sweetheart."

At switchback nineteen, I heard again the rumble of rocks being swept over the edge, torn out of the ground by the wheels going over them. I cried out in panic, imagining us following the rocks over the edge.

"Sweetheart, we're fine."

I glared at him. "Don't you dare 'sweetheart' me again." I swallowed hard, pushing down my angry words. "We never should have driven this goddamn road."

The view from the top of the plateau *was* magnificent. It was as if we had arrived in a little Scottish village with small, neatly built homes and tidy gardens among the large dark-green Mopani trees. A big redbrick church, named after the Scottish missionary David Livingstone, had a faded green tin roof and bell tower. But I knew I wasn't in Scotland when I read the billboard:

AVOID HIV/AIDS

"ABSTAIN OR BE FAITHFUL IN MARRIAGE"

"JIKORANI PANJI GOMEZGEKANI PA NATHENGWA"

CCCP SYNOD OF LIVINGSTONIA

A small, slender man who looked about twenty-five introduced himself as Chiso at the church. His neatly pressed blue striped shirt looked two sizes too big for him. He sent a young boy on a bicycle to fetch a key so we could enter the church. A few minutes later, I stood on the brick floor of the church and looked up at the large stained-glass window over the entrance that dominated the church. I presumed David Livingstone was the white man in the center of the stained-glass window, dressed in a brown waistcoat over a white shirt, one hand on his hip, the other hand reaching out to the half-naked Black man holding a spear. Several other Black men stood bowed on either side of him.

I thought of the adage I'd heard Black people quote: "We've got the Bible, and they've got the land."

Later that day, we purchased a mushroom the size of a dinner plate for supper. At our campsite, Tom began to prepare the mushroom, but on closer inspection, we saw that hundreds of small, gray, wriggling worms had beaten us to it and were enjoying the mushroom for their supper. Not up to eating a mushroom with worms, we simply sat on the edge of the plateau overlooking the lush green valley below. With the moonlight glistening on the lake in the distance and diamonds of stars just beginning to appear, we clinked our wine glasses. "To the worms. May they enjoy our supper," said Tom.

"Can you believe it? It's exactly three months since we arrived in

Johannesburg, and so much has happened since then," I said. A little glowworm was slowly inching its way up my bare leg.

Tom raised his glass to the sky. "This is a geologist's dream, sitting here overlooking the Rift Valley. That's something to celebrate as well."

The glowworm stopped on my knee. I reached out and touched it with my index finger, and as fast as a glowworm can run, it made its escape and disappeared into the bush. "I'm glad we don't have to go back down that road," I said.

"Going down will be easier," said Tom. "We'll go back down that road. The other way is much longer." Tom stood up and told me he was going to make himself a peanut butter sandwich.

"I don't want to go back on that road again."

He paused and turned around. "We'll be fine."

However, by morning, Tom had convinced me the descent would be easier and safer than the ascent. I can't imagine why I believed that.

Going down, I felt as if I were on a roller coaster on the downward run.

"Slow down. Slow down," I said repeatedly.

"I can't go any slower. If I take my foot off the accelerator, we'll just stop. Just close your eyes."

I shut my eyes. Suddenly the Cruiser stopped, and I heard, "Oh shit."

I opened my eyes to see a truck facing us. "We're not going to be able to pass it," I said in disbelief.

A young man jumped out of the truck and began directing the truck driver to reverse up against the rocky cliff side as much as possible. When the truck driver couldn't pull in any closer to the rocks, his passenger waved his arms at us, indicating to Tom to come forward. The truck driver reached out and pulled in his side mirrors. Tom pulled in his side mirror.

"You won't get past him," I said. For once, I even dared to look down to the valley below. "Oh, God." Panic gripped me.

Tom clenched the steering wheel and leaned forward. "I'll get past," he murmured.

Tom went forward with only inches between the two vehicles and a few inches between our wheels and the precipitous drop to the valley bottom. The rumble of stones and rocks set free began as soon as Tom slowly drove toward the man directing him. I held my breath and focused on the edge of the track and the man waving his arms directing Tom. Tom inched forward slowly alongside the idling truck and its escaping diesel fumes. I urged Tom, "Go closer to the truck." I heard the rumble of stones breaking free and tumbling over the edge. Finally, I could breathe, and Tom waved a thank-you to the man who had guided him.

"You'd better learn to trust my instincts," I said. "We're just damn lucky it happened near the bottom of the road. We wouldn't have been able to pass them if it had happened higher up."

He nodded his head. "Yes. You were right. I should've listened to you. We should've gone the safer route." He turned to look at me. "I'm so sorry. It won't happen again."

I thought of him always making the important decisions in our marriage and wondered how we would break that pattern and live as equal partners. I needed to trust my gut instincts and not just always agree with him.

Back at the lake's edge, we headed for the bar on the beach. Pink, purple, red, and white lacy bras hung above the counter of the wooden shack. Some volunteer youngsters had probably left the bras there after a few wild parties. Tourists had yet to discover this beach, and bras were a luxury item for the local women in these parts. A young boy leaned against the grubby counter of the shack, scratching his crotch. He looked disinterested in life and hardly glanced my way. He wore a faded blue shirt with "Boston" blazed across the front, probably given to him by a volunteer. As I stood in the lake sipping my warm bottle of orange Fanta, cool waves swirled around my knees.

Malawi is a safe and beautiful country and an easy step into Africa. We saw young American and European volunteers at almost every turn. A hedonist's playground for these idealistic foreigners. In countries with risks and dangers, we saw only the heavy hitters, such as Doctors Without Borders (MSF) and the Red Cross, as well as United Nations agencies and peacekeepers.

Near the Malawi-Tanzania border, we stopped in Karonga to buy some battery water. We parked and walked across the dirt road to a building whose sign read CHIPETUPETU COFFIN AND BATTERY WORK-SHOP. Two men stood on the veranda. The younger man dressed in a colorful kaftan chiseled a wood plank; the other leaned against a pillar, a cigarette dangling from his lips. On the workbench was a small, unfinished wood coffin. They greeted us and said, yes, they had battery fluid. The man with the cigarette disappeared into the building.

"How's business?" Tom asked the man in the kaftan. The man held a mallet in his calloused right hand, and in his left, he had a hammer. The sun shone on the fine light brown sawdust sprinkled in his black hair.

The man let his arms drop to his side. "Coffin business good." He smiled, but his sad eyes told another story. He patted the small coffin beside him. I pondered on his mood of resignation and his apparent acceptance of the inevitability of death, even the death of a child. Like many African countries, Malawi is significantly impacted by the horrors of HIV and AIDS. Over two million Africans would die of AIDS during the year of our trip. How many deaths and how much suffering would have been avoided if the political and religious voices of Europe and America had promoted, rather than condemned, the use of condoms to prevent the spread of HIV and AIDS? I struggled, as I so often did, to understand the injustices of the world and my silence about them.

The following day we pulled into the Malawi border post and had our car and ourselves stamped out of the country. On the Tanzanian

side, a grumpy border official insisted we purchase third-party insurance from him. Because we already had insurance, we refused. But
the official insisted again. Like scrapping children, we argued with the
grumpy man. He waved his official document around in the air like
a flag. After fifteen minutes of haggling in the baking sun, he finally
agreed to let us cross the border, "but just this one time."

He wrote our information in pen in his logbook—passport
details, dates of birth, places of birth, citizenships, occupations—and
asked for the name of the hotel where we'd be staying.

"Best Western," Tom replied. He didn't know any names of hotels
in Dar es Salaam and assumed that neither did the border official.
Tanzania, our sixth country, as it turned out, would become the first
country where we felt the need to seek safety in a hotel.

Chapter 9
What Really Matters in Life

Tanzania, 2005

Once in Tanzania, we headed toward Dar es Salaam, a city with a population of three million. We arrived in the evening to chaos, confusion, and traffic like nothing I'd ever experienced. Beaten-up cars, diesel-belching trucks, buses overloaded with people both inside and hanging on to the outside, luggage piled high on the roof, and all competing for space. No one used turn signals, traffic lights seemed to be for ambiance only, and the driver with the biggest bull bar won.

Tom navigated, yelling out directions. "Move into the right lane. Hell no, go left."

Sirens wailed, car alarms screamed, brakes screeched, police whistled, and every exhaust pipe sounded as if it had a hole in it. I could hardly breathe the foul air of diesel fumes.

"Turn right now. Shit, it's one-way. Keep going straight."

Impatient drivers blasted hooters, and traffic paused for several seconds while vehicles rearranged themselves on the road.

"Watch that guy on your right; he's about to make a move somewhere."

The Cruiser's brake system was dangerously overheating as I constantly slammed on the brakes to avoid yet another collision. Truck engines revved, and buses skidded while passengers risked life and limb to jump on or off them while the vehicles continued moving. I felt my adrenaline pumping, and I started to feel aggressive. Soon I was one with all the other drivers, swerving as pedestrians dashed and cyclists weaved into the road. "Shit, that was close," I said.

Yet there was order in all the confusion. The traffic did move; we just weren't sure of the final destination. We had no map, only the latitude and longitude coordinates of a campsite on the other side of this densely populated city. It grew dark. We had been on the road for over two hours, and by now, signs of some kind of boisterous party had begun to spring up all around us. We were totally lost. We watched as police put up barricades across some roads.

"There's got be something going on," I said. "There're police and military everywhere."

"Just keep going north until we're out of this chaos."

We left the city lights and continued north. Soon we found ourselves driving deeper and deeper into a slum area. Potholed dirt roads replaced tar; tin shacks replaced buildings, and people swayed and wobbled onto the street. Women huddled around pots of steaming food balanced over flickering fires.

I swerved to avoid some children kicking a ball. "What should I do?" I asked.

Men surged toward our car. "Turn around," Tom insisted.

"When?"

"Fuck, now!" he yelled as several drunken, screaming men surrounded our car and tried to open the doors.

I slammed the car into reverse, did a quick U-turn, and headed back toward the city center. Meanwhile, Tom scrambled through his GPS coordinates to find a hotel for the night. After what seemed an eternity, we arrived at the Sea Cliffs Hotel on the Indian Ocean. A smartly dressed young man at the reception desk shuffled papers. He chatted to a woman behind us until Tom interrupted their animated discussion and asked if a room was available. The receptionist beamed as he slid a form across the counter for us to complete. "You lucky we have a room for you. Many, many very important people are here."

In our room, we turned on the television and watched Tanzanians celebrating the inauguration of Jakaya Kikwete, the fourth president of Tanzania. Many African heads of state and other dignitaries were in Dar es Salaam to witness his swearing-in.

We also had something significant to celebrate; we had crossed Africa from west to east. We had left the cold and stormy Atlantic Ocean on the west coast just over three months earlier. Now we stood on our balcony and watched the warm tropical waves of the Indian Ocean on the east coast.

"Next coast, the Mediterranean Sea," I said.

Tom suggested we celebrate and have "our own party all alone," but we were not alone: mosquitoes gate-crashed our celebration. We did our best to ignore them and focused on the scene before us—lights from shipping boats reflected off the waves. On the beach, fishermen hauled in their boats, and in the distance, we heard the sounds of drumming and joyful celebrations.

I felt a sense of achievement. Never could I have imagined how alive all the challenges—chaotic driving, complex negotiations, language struggles, eating unrecognizable food, sleeping in strange places—would make me feel. I thrived in this new lifestyle. Tom and I had done more together in the last three months than we had done together in the previous three years.

While in Dar, we planned to apply for visas for Egypt and Sudan. Rumor had it that a Sudan visa could take six weeks, so we braced ourselves for a long wait.

After an interview with the counselor at the Egyptian embassy, we had our visas for Egypt within twenty-four hours.

The Sudanese high commissioner welcomed us into his office but abruptly explained, "You must have two reference letters from Sudanese people living in Sudan."

"That's not possible, sir," Tom said. "We don't know anybody in Sudan."

He pushed our visa applications back across his desk toward us and said, "Then you need to get a letter of introduction from the Canadian government. It will speed up your application."

"We don't write letters," the person behind the counter at the Canadian embassy informed us. Eventually, they agreed and wrote a letter that stated we were driving to Cairo and that they had no reason to disbelieve our claim.

Back at the Sudanese embassy, we handed in all the required documentation and the letter. The following day we received our Sudanese visas.

I mistakenly believed that nothing could stop us from reaching our goal: the shores of the Mediterranean Sea. I was wrong.

Before we left Dar es Salaam, there was one more place to explore: the Zanzibar archipelago, which lies forty-six miles from the Tanzanian shoreline. The best-known and most exotic island of the archipelago is informally known as Zanzibar; the official name is Unguja Island, and Stone Town is the capital. We decided to leave the Cruiser on the mainland and take the ferry to the island of Zanzibar.

While rushing to catch our ferry from Dar es Salaam to Zanzibar, an official-looking man called Tom aside and told him he had to pay a $10 port tax.

"Give me a receipt," I said. The man ignored me and continued to harass Tom. "The lady at the ticket office said we didn't have to pay a port tax," I continued.

The official glared at us, and not wanting to get into an argument or be late for the ferry, Tom handed the man $10.

"That's a rip-off, and you fell for it," I told him.

"What's with you? This is not the time or place to get into an argument."

"That man's tongue is a bag of lies!" I said. But we agreed that I would handle the tickets on the return journey.

Several days later, as we entered through the ferry terminal gates, several touts approached us, each jockeying for Tom's attention, each offering him "a special deal" on the return tickets.

They ignored me and continued to jostle around Tom. Leaving Tom alone with the touts, I headed to the numerous ticket kiosks and purchased our tickets. With the tickets held high, I yelled, "I've got the tickets, Tom."

The touts glared at Tom in disbelief and disgust. "You are not a real man," they said and stormed off.

"They just had a little lesson in women's lib," said Tom. He told me of the animated conversation he'd had with them. He couldn't convince them that I would buy the tickets without his approval and permission. Confused, they began to ask probing questions about our relationship. Could Tom bring home people for supper without first asking me? Could he force himself on me to have sex? Despite Tom's explanations about women's rights, the men remained skeptical and not convinced that I would buy the tickets without my husband's approval.

Tom and I struggled to navigate the assigned gender roles of the societies in which we had lived. Obviously, Tom was bigger and stronger than me, so physically, he could do things I couldn't. However, I'd taken on many roles and responsibilities I would never have considered necessary in Canada.

During our long drive, Tom and I had to throw out many traditionally accepted gender roles. We determined who was best suited for each task. In the cities, I drove, and Tom navigated. When dealing with officials and when patience was required, Tom took over. When asking locals for help, I was in charge. The barriers we had built between us over the years were beginning to slowly crumble.

The ancient Stone Town, the old part of Zanzibar City, influenced by African, Arabian Peninsula, Indian, and European cultures over the last millennium, looked tired. We wandered through the narrow, winding alleyways. Due to years of neglect, the stone buildings built with coral rocks showed signs of decay and erosion. The once-glorious white walls had been washed gray over time. We stopped to admire the large wooden doors—ornate, heavy, and adorned with copper knobs, a sign of the merchants' wealth in the old days of trading in ivory, spices, and slaves. Women dressed in hijabs and chadors walked briskly past us as they headed to the market. Children laughing and playing followed behind. Men wearing traditional Muslim *kofias*, small skullcaps worn as a sign of respect, stood in groups chatting loudly, sharing the day's news.

We stopped for a drink of freshly squeezed sugar cane juice from cane grown on the island. A man fed the cane stalks into the press and turned by hand a large blue wheel, which crushed the cane stalk. The creamy-colored liquid ran into a tin basin; an assistant scooped up the liquid with a green plastic cup and poured it into a glass. I drank the warm, sweet juice and passed the glass to Tom for his drink. When Tom finished, the assistant rinsed the glass and gave it to the person next in line. Nothing was thoroughly washed. So much for all my health and cleanliness concerns, now simply being washed away by sweet sugar cane. Even my immune system was being kicked into high gear and made to work hard.

The mosque minaret boomed into life as the muezzin called faithful Muslims to worship. Seagulls resting on the radio antennas and TV aerials around the mosque minaret seemed unperturbed, no doubt used to the sound since Muslims are called to prayer five times a day.

In the market, restless pigeons and chickens in wire-mesh cages waited to be sold, fruits and vegetables to be weighed and placed into bags for sale. The smell of fresh and dried fish mingled with the sweet temptations of spices, and cats prowled beneath the stalls, waiting for throwaway fish entrails.

We stood in the shade of a large poinsettia tree in full bloom, our only reminder of the Christmas we were missing in Calgary that day.

After resting briefly, we followed a chopping sound until we came to a shirtless man with a large axe in his calloused muscular hand, whacking thick, hard logs. He was making a *ngalawa*, a sailboat.

As we watched the boat maker's powerful and chiseled arms glistening in the sun, Tom smiled and said, "Now, that's raw muscular power."

The grains of hot sand burned my bare feet as we walked along the white beach where young boys played soccer, men strolled together, and discarded plastic water bottles lay trapped in the seaweed. Waves lapped at the edge of wood dugouts on the beach. Across the sheltered bay, luxurious yachts and cruise boats were anchored alongside wooden dhows and colorful, rusting fishing boats, both large and small.

"Let's have lunch before we visit the old Anglican church," Tom said. I agreed, knowing that when Tom's hungry, he needs to eat, or else he'll drag himself behind me like a lost shadow. The aroma of spicy cooking wafted from a nearby stall, and we stopped and each bought a *mishkaki* (a spicy chicken shish kebab) and several *vitumbras* (small rice pancakes flavored with cardamom and coconut). Although crispy on the outside, the *vitumbras* melted in my mouth.

The British began building the Anglican church in 1873 on the site of the largest slave market on the east coast of Africa. That same year, Britain and Zanzibar had signed a treaty agreeing to suppress slavery. Once Zanzibar became a British protectorate in 1897, slavery was technically abolished. More than 3.3 million Africans were sent to their tragic fate from this single slave market. There are no estimates of how many died making the journey to Zanzibar: they remain the untold stories and the forgotten dead. Only the Africans who arrived at the final destination were thought worthy enough to be counted.

Slave traders hacked and slashed their way into the interior of Africa. African chiefs sold, traded, and trafficked captured prisoners from tribes they had fought. Slave traders kidnapped, bribed, plundered, and pillaged villages. They forced men, women, and children to walk thousands of perilous miles to Bagamoyo, a town on the coast of the Indian Ocean, a journey many did not survive, dying along the way from starvation, injuries, diseases such as malaria, and sheer exhaustion. Captured men were also forced to carry mammoth elephant tusks for the ivory trade, among other loot. Their final African destination, should they survive the trip to Bagamoyo, would be the island of Zanzibar. From there, they were shipped mainly to the West Indies and the Caribbean.

I forced myself to look at the monument outside the church: five life-size figures chiseled out of dark brown stone, the original chains used during the slave trade hung around their necks. They stood silently in the concrete pit, but I swear I could hear their hearts beating inside the stone. I searched for the words to express my horror, but there were none; all I could do was imagine their painful, unspoken words.

Inside the church, I looked up at the stained-glass windows divided into three separate panels. In the middle panel, a bent Black man stood with his back to the church, and in each side panel stood a tall white saint looking at the man. Not even the sun shone through those windows.

In front of the altar, a red circle on the floor marked the exact position of the pole to which slaves were tied before being sold. Their bodies were whipped in a frenzy of lashings because the slaves that didn't cry out loudly could be sold for a higher price. Some slaves earned such a high price that the slave trader would throw in a child for free.

Captured slaves were held in two separate chambers, one for men and the other for women and children. I entered one of the dark, dank chambers, with its low ceiling of logs and mud. Pillars held up the roof. Around the room ran a hard bench, high enough off the ground so that my feet didn't reach the ground below when I sat on

it. On the floor, tunnels opened up into the sea. At high tide, waves
flooded the floor below and washed feces and other human waste out
to sea. I imagined the stench. I placed my hands on the ceiling only
eight inches above my head, then clutched the cold, rusted chain still
attached to a pillar and wept.

A chill of horror flowed through me. I thought about the similar-
ity between slavery and apartheid: both insidious yet cruel systems of
racial discrimination based solely on the color of one's skin.

My thoughts turned to the anti-apartheid freedom fighters who
had risked prison and even their lives in the struggle to end apartheid
and free Black and other non-white South Africans. For over three
hundred years, except for a few, most Europeans and Americans also
turned their backs on the horrors of the slave trade.

As I sat in the Zanzibar slave chambers, I felt chilled, knowing
there had probably been few survivors of that nightmarish system.
A few were buried; others waited for death. For most, death came
through brutal treatment, either thrown overboard or whipped on
plantations. They were stripped of their humanity and reduced to
nothing more than the walking dead.

I left the slave chambers and walked out into the warm sunlight,
thinking of how easily those with power brainwashed ordinary people.
With the benefit of new insight, I became aware of how easily I had
been manipulated and controlled. But if growing older had taught me
anything, it was the necessity to keep learning and improving. With
this new awareness, I committed whenever the opportunity to combat
injustice arose. I resolved to always do the morally right thing, regardless of the possible outcomes.

Leaving Zanzibar and Dar es Salaam, we headed north to the village of Bagamoyo on the mainland, where the captured slaves waited
to be taken to Zanzibar. The dirt track wove through tall grass and
dense bush. A large brown puff adder moved silently across the road
while black-and-orange starlings swooped overhead to catch flying

insects. As we jostled along the dusty track, it felt like old times again, the peaceful and unhurried Africa I loved.

As we rounded a bend, we spotted in the distance a crowd of people standing on the track. I approached them slowly. They made no attempt to move out of our way, so I stopped about twenty feet from the crowd. Some squatted while others stood around a wooden box. The box sat on a mat in the shade of a canopy strung across the track and held up by four poles.

"What are they doing?" Tom asked. We watched as smartly dressed women, men in ill-fitting suits, and hushed children turned and looked at us. Tom got out of the Cruiser and hesitated, unsure of what to do. A middle-aged man with tired eyes slowly walked toward Tom as if carrying a heavy load. I watched them both shake hands, not forcefully, just a gentle touch.

"It is my mother's funeral," the man said. "She died," he added, as if he had to explain the need for the funeral.

An old gray-haired man with a beard approached Tom. They shook hands, and the man introduced himself as the preacher. "We will move the coffin so you can pass," he said.

"Yes," said the first man. "We can move my mother so you can pass." He looked at the ground as if sadness would swallow him up.

Tom waved his hand. "No, no, not necessary, we can wait. We can go back." The bush was too dense for us to bushwhack around the mourners. Unable to convince them that we would wait, Tom asked if we could pay our respects to the man's mother. The preacher nodded and put his arm around the shoulders of the broken man. They turned to walk back. After walking a short distance, I stopped beside the wooden coffin. Flowers had been spread across the top, and a dainty blue dragonfly with transparent wings rested on one of the pink flowers. I bowed my head, closed my eyes, and wished the deceased well on her next journey.

Tom and I returned to the Cruiser and, under a sunny sky,

watched as the men tenderly picked up the handmade wooden coffin and moved it with care to the side of the track. They untied the gray canopy and dragged it into the bush. They rolled up the grass mat and moved the flowers and ornaments. Then the men, women, and children stood silently to the side so we could pass.

Watching them made me think about my death, my funeral. I realized that it wasn't death that I feared; it was the emptiness of life. I thought of the question I had asked myself that set me on this journey—what would I do if I had one year to live? I thought of the young cancer patient, Annie, dying alone, and wondered about the old woman in the coffin surrounded by family and friends. How gently they had moved her coffin to the side of the road, how ordinary it seemed to them that life goes on after death.

I broke the silence in the car. "It doesn't matter if I don't reach Cairo."

"What do you mean?" Tom asked.

"I'm not sure. It just seems so unimportant now whether I get there. This," I said, pointing to the people, "makes me wonder what really matters in my life."

As we drove slowly past the crowd, I looked down at the coffin. I felt as if the dead woman had touched me, reached out, grabbed my soul, and given me a good shake. I needed that reminder.

I wanted meaning in my life and people that mattered, not another "done that" ticked off my list. I thought of my sons, Derek and David, and how much I loved and missed them. I wondered if I mattered to them. I hoped I mattered to Tom. How could I show him he mattered to me? I didn't even know where to start.

As we rounded a bend in the track, the funeral scene disappeared from our sight. I thought of the wails of grief at the time of death and the cries of life at the time of birth. As a midwife, I loved to hear the cries of a newborn, to see the mother's tears of joy, and I remembered the tiny, clenched fists of infants. An African midwife once told me, in those little fists, "the baby, they each bring a new gift to the world." What a gift the woman in the coffin had given me when she left the world. "Treasure your relationships," she had whispered. As she set me on a new path and destination, I would forever hold her wisdom close.

I thought of the people we'd met and who had touched me on our journey—the old woman in the coffin, the Malawi man who made us a bolt, the Zambian teacher. They had all taught me something about the richness of life and the value of meaningful relationships and community. Africa had become my home once more and was again my wise and gentle teacher.

Chapter 10
A Quintessential Africa

Tanzania, 2005

In the village of Bagamoyo on the shores of the Indian Ocean, I walked around the twenty-three-foot-wide bottle-shaped trunk of Africa's giant "soul tree"—the baobab. Growing up in South Africa, I read that some called the baobab the upside-down tree because God had pulled the tree out in anger and thrown it back into the ground upside down. The branches look like roots and can grow as high as a five-story building. Others say crocodiles will not attack you if you soak the baobab's seeds in water and drink the potion. The San people believe there are spirits in the tree's flowers and that if you pick one, you will be torn apart by a lion. The large mystical white blossoms open only in the shadow of the moonlight, so to witness one opening is rare. The five-petal—nearly eight inches wide—flower only blooms for twenty-four hours.

I ran my hands over the rough, elephant-like bark of the gigantic tree. If only the spirits that lived in this tree could talk. They had witnessed the thousands of farmers, fishermen, spiritual leaders, chiefs, hunters, trackers, herders, warriors, teachers, traditional healers, and mothers with infants and children arriving as captured slaves. Torn from their tribal cultures, languages, communities, and families and crammed into dingy dungeons, these bewildered victims waited to be transported in overcrowded dhows to Zanzibar and later sold to the highest bidder at the slave market.

Is Bagamoyo where the slaves had their hearts ripped out in

96

hopelessness? Is this why Bagamoyo means "lay down your heart" in Swahili? Standing still with my hand on the bark, I imagined that the spirits of the baobab trees must have wept at the cruelty that humans unleashed on one another.

I hadn't come to see the baobab but rather the unimposing small white building next to it. Above the entrance is a sign with the words THROUGH THIS DOOR, DR. DAVID LIVINGSTONE PASSED. We had come here to see where Dr. Livingstone's body had rested before it made the journey to Zanzibar and then back home to Britain. His heart never made it back home, however. When he died of malaria and dysentery in Zambia, Britain demanded that his body be returned to London. But the demand met with opposition. "Dr. Livingstone's heart belongs to Africa," his devoted followers Susi and Chuma declared. They sliced open the explorer's chest, removed his heart, and buried it beneath a muvule tree in the Zambian village of Illala. Then they dried out his body before carrying it ninety-nine miles to the town of Bagamoyo, which had become the main trading port for ivory and slaves.

As a child reading about the explorer, I was enthralled by Livingstone. The legendary Scottish missionary and medical doctor arrived in Southern Africa in 1841 at twenty-eight. He explored the interior of Africa, searching for the source of the Nile River, and was the first white man to reach the Mosi-oa-Tunya—"the smoke that thunders"—waterfalls in Zimbabwe. Immediately, he renamed them Victoria Falls after his queen. In the 1960s, in what was then called Rhodesia, I had stood at the foot of his imposing statue, which claimed that Livingstone had discovered Victoria Falls. The indigenous people who knew it was there long before Dr. Livingstone apparently did not discover them. That honor, according to the British, "belonged to Dr. David Livingstone."

What beliefs had I tattooed onto my inner being about the world and my own life? Which stubborn and ill-founded opinions and beliefs had bulldozed through my relationship with Tom, nearly tearing us apart? Were these beliefs, opinions, and views related? I began to question every thought I had. I wanted to scrub myself clean, to rid myself of those external and internal misperceptions and prejudices that pulled me down or led me astray. I wondered what I was truly searching for and in which direction I should steer the rest of my life. I saw no clear answers, only the need to keep asking questions.

After parking among tall palm trees on New Year's Day, we walked down to the beach. The rising sun glistened off the waves, seagulls screeched above, and in the distance, I saw six small dhows returning from their night's work, their white sails fluttering in the early morning breeze. I had no idea what 2006 held in store for me. But I knew, as clearly as it is possible to know anything, that lives—mine, Tom's, and others—would soon be changed forever.

Kenya, 2006

Although Mount Kilimanjaro, Africa's highest mountain, is in Tanzania, the best view of the mountain with animals in the foreground is from Kenya, so we crossed into Kenya.

While sipping iced drinks on the veranda of a luxurious lodge in Tsavo National Park, we watched the wildlife around the watering hole below. Mount Kilimanjaro loomed above the clouds, the sun setting behind its snowcapped peak, with zebras, giraffes, antelope, elephants, and warthogs taking a refreshing drink in its shadow. This was a moment to be savored, a glimpse of quintessential Africa.

We came to the Tsavo National Park to see the large, notorious, maneless man-eating Tsavo lions, whose only predators are humans. As darkness descended, we snuck out of the lodge and, against the rules—no driving after dark—headed for the campsite. Because of the danger of hitting wildlife, we drove slowly with our bright spotlights on.

A man at the campsite, perhaps a ranger, waved a large stick at us. "You can't drive at night; it's too dangerous," he said.

Dangerous? I thought. Dangerous is pitching a tent on a moonless night in an unfenced and unsecured campsite, alone, with a stick-wielding man, in known man-eating-lion territory. We assured the man we had stopped for the night, and I scanned the trees with my flashlight for the familiar glint of leopard eyes. It was my job to be on the lookout while Tom pitched the tent.

"Hurry up," I muttered. "The mosquitos are eating me alive."

"You're lucky that's the only thing eating you right now," he said.

The early morning hours brought out all the usual animals. But what delighted us when we alighted from our vehicle at an observation point was the migration of thousands of buffalo, moving steadily across the African savannah. The air filled with their contented mooing and grunting. Dust stirred by the thundering hooves swirled in the morning sunbeams. Startled out of the tall grass, guinea fowls protesting screamed, "*kek, kaaa, ke kaaa*"—which sounds like "come back, come back"—before escaping up into the air. Captivated by the sights and sounds in the valley below, we stood beside a sign that read LEAVE YOUR VEHICLE AT YOUR OWN RISK. African-savannah buffalos, which can weigh up to one ton, are highly unpredictable and dangerous, and their only predators are lions and humans.

After about half an hour of hypnotic buffalo watching, we returned to our Cruiser and began our search again for the elusive Tsavo lions. After a few feet of driving, Tom stopped.

I leaned over to see what Tom was looking at and was stunned to see five large Tsavo lions with two cubs relaxing under a wild fig tree within a few feet from where we had stood watching the buffalo.

"We're lucky we weren't their breakfast," Tom said without taking his eyes off the lions.

"I'd never have gotten out of the car if I'd known the lions were that close." I looked back to where we came from. "They knew we were there." I gave a nervous laugh.

Tom nodded. "Yep. They smelled us for sure."

The lion and four lionesses were larger, paler in color, and their coats smoother than those of other lions we'd seen. The Tsavo lion's mane was indeed largely missing—another bad hair day. In the early morning sun, we watched the lions resting in the shade of the tree. As I rolled down my window and breathed in the smell of lion, grass, and dust, I listened to the whistling song, "*chleeo, chleeo*," of a lone crowned hornbill bird in a branch above.

The Tsavo lions got their reputation as man-eaters when, in 1897, the British, scrambling to control Africa, began building a railway line along the same transportation corridor as the slave-trade route—from Mombasa on the Indian Ocean to Kisumu on Lake Victoria in the interior. Just west of Kilimanjaro in the Tsavo area, building progress was hampered when a significant number of railroad laborers were killed and eaten by lions. Perhaps the lions had developed a taste for human flesh when weak slaves, unable to keep up, were left to die en route.

In 1897, hunters finally shot and killed the "man-eating" Tsavo lions. This unquestioned killing came to define the European relationship with the continent. Today hunters and poachers continue to slaughter the wildlife, mainly for their valuable body parts but also as recreational trophies to take home for their walls and mantels. Biologists predict that by the end of the century, more than half of all African wildlife species will be extinct. As an African proverb puts it: "Until the lion learns how to write, every story will glorify the hunter."

Tragically, future generations will never experience the wildlife we've witnessed. Humans are destroying the animals' habitats and hunting and poaching all wildlife into extinction. Biologists estimate that by 2025, elephants could be completely extinct in the wild. As for the lions, hundreds of thousands once roamed the savannah of Africa, but today there are fewer than twenty thousand, and the majority are in wildlife preserves. An indescribable ache tore at my heart when I realized and had to begin to accept that the wild Africa I had experienced as a child was no more.

Beside our Cruiser, the little cubs played with a wide-eyed yellow chameleon that had wandered across their path. A lioness stretched with her bum in the air and yawned. The lion rolled over; she walked over to him and rubbed against him before lying down once more to rest in the shade. After an hour, we rolled up our windows and bid the lions farewell.

Tanzania, 2006

Africa's borders taught us patience, especially at the smaller border crossings where officials seemed less aggressive. We often had to wait for an official to arrive. Returning to Tanzania, however, was smooth. The border official smiled as he completed the form and stamped our Carnet de Passages, a legal document required to take vehicles across a border. In only a few generations, colonists had left behind a vast legacy of bureaucracy. Written in baffling English legalese despite its French name, the Carnet de Passages is a vehicle's own passport. The carnet challenges those who don't read English or who don't own glasses to read the small print. The Arab border officials, who read right to left, had our Cruiser stamped out of the country when we entered and stamped into the country when we left. At the end of the trip, the carnet is returned to the same office that issued it, adorned with official stamps to prove the vehicle is back in the country of registration. It's a bureaucratic circus, and the Carnet de Passages was the most regularly forged document we saw. We often completed the forms ourselves at the border and then set off to find someone with a stamp. The excuses we heard for the man with the stamp being unavailable included: "he is at church," "he lives in the other village," "he has gone for malaria treatment," "he is sleeping now," and "he is at a funeral." Next time, we vowed to take our own stamps.

The words "Ngorongoro" and "Serengeti" rolled off my tongue—national wildlife parks I had dreamed of visiting. Standing on the rim of the Ngorongoro volcanic caldera, I felt as if I had stopped at the edge of the earth. Growing up, one of my favorite people in the world was Joy Adamson, a passionate wildlife advocate, a naturalist, and the author of *Born Free*. Her story of raising a wild orphaned cub, whom she named Elsa, in the wilderness fascinated me. She epitomized everything I wished to become.

The official at the gate to the road going into the Ngorongoro Crater told us we had to take a guide along. But our newly acquired skill of persuading officials to allow us to proceed against rules soon had the man waving us through the gate without a guide. The narrow, rutted dirt road wound down through the densely forested rim, dropping two hundred feet to the crater floor, opening to grassland and a world of wildlife wonders.

We stopped under a thorny acacia tree; the earth was scorched dry. Lack of rain is advantageous only to the tourist since it is easier to spot wildlife when the trees are bare and the grass is dying. Hearing singing voices behind us, we turned to see about thirty Maasai women dressed in royal blue walking down the road we had just driven. They sang and danced; their performance was a plea for rain from their ancestors and God. Following the women were local Maasai herdsmen armed only with spears and arrows and hundreds of anxious-looking cows. They were making their way down into the grazing lands where zebras, buffalo, wildebeests, and antelope awaited them. The Maasai people were allowed to graze their cattle in the conservation area, including the Ngorongoro Crater. They had protested that they'd been pushed out of their traditional grassing area by the formation of the parks.

Hundreds of wildebeests—ungainly looking animals that are easily spooked—grazed in the distance. Hundreds of cunning zebras mingled among the wildebeests, knowing that lions, should they appear, prefer a wildebeest over a zebra for lunch.

A giraffe (the world's tallest animal) and her calf nibbled on the leaves of an acacia, their favorite tree, despite the large thorns on the branches. Giraffes are docile animals but will defend themselves and can even kill a lion with a sharp forward kick of their forelegs.

We parked under a mimosa tree beside a small water hole to have lunch. I sat on the roof of our Cruiser, watching the elephants drink. Starlings, African kites, and weavers soared around the water's edges as fish eagles perched on the branch of a fig tree. Near the water, a little gray vervet monkey played with a large round ball of elephant dung. He rolled it, tried to eat it, pushed it, and then sat on it. We listened to the melancholic howls of jackals and the laughing barks of spotted hyenas in the distance.

Later we watched a lioness, crouched low, slink slowly toward the unsuspecting wildebeests and zebras. She paused, alert, then slowly began sinking her belly onto the ground. Her chest heaved, her ears twitched, her tail flicked, and her gaze locked on the passing prey. Suddenly a baboon cry from the acacia tree alerted the wildebeests and zebras to the danger, and the stampede began, with four lionesses in pursuit. The fleeing prey dodged and weaved in desperate attempts to escape the grip of the lionesses' paws and powerful jaws. Amid dust and screams, a killing struggle was on, and then, as abruptly as it had started, the hunt was over.

At the day's end, we left the crater floor and drove back up the caldera to our campsite. Sweaty and dusty, I was looking forward to a shower. But a sign saying CLOSED NO WATER hung across the shower-room entrance. Elephants had beaten me to the water and had emptied the camp's water supply.

Except for the company of a troop of olive baboons, we were alone at the campsite that night. Despite the absence of a fence around the campsite, a sign read, STAY IN CAMPSITE BECAUSE WILD ANIMAL MAY ATTACK HUMANS. Tom and I sat quietly watching the baboons, creatures that can be aggressive but are also particularly entertaining to observe. This troop seemed disinterested in us. Infants clung to their mothers while curious youngsters explored their surroundings. The male baboons strutted about, yawned, and bared their large, canine-like teeth. The females groomed one another, eating the bugs or ticks they removed from their hairy coats. We heard the baboons' low, cough-like grunts as they moved through the grass. At one point, a large male baboon picked up a scorpion and carefully flicked the stinger off before eating his crunchy meal.

The evening was peaceful, and I was in a world I loved. Surely, we are meant to live in nature. When I leave the wilderness, I always feel I've left behind part of whom I was meant to be. But almost as soon as I had returned to the wilderness of my youth, I knew I had to let go of my African dreams and accept a new reality. My world now was a different one. And even Africa was changing. Just like the continent, I couldn't live in the past. I had to look forward, not backward. Besides, already on this trip, I had seen more of Africa than most people will ever witness. I needed to embrace that fact and not hunger for experiences I could never have.

At the break of dawn, we were up and back on the road heading north. Our destination: the largest lake in Africa—Lake Victoria. Traveling along the shoreline, we stopped at villages to chat with the locals, many of them fishermen. The colonists introduced alien Nile perch into the lake in the early 1950s. Since then, the monster fishes have eaten the indigenous fish and destroyed the natural habitat, creating an ecological catastrophe. Local fishermen struggle to make a living. They cannot compete with modern fishing corporations that catch the perch, then wash, clean, and fillet them before shipping considerable quantities to Europe.

"What is that smell?" I asked a woman selling vegetables. She shrugged and said she didn't know. Perhaps she had grown accustomed to the putrid fish heads sold in the markets. It seemed ironic and disheartening that the fish fillets are exported to fill the bellies of those on the other side of the ocean, yet the locals struggle to feed their families. Later we learned that planes fly to Europe with the fish fillets. The locals told us that "planes bring back other stuff." I imagined what that stuff was. Again, the cold reality hit me: Africa's resources continue to be exploited by foreign companies. Is this the face of neocolonialism?

The Tanzanian Tourist Association informed us that the road to Rwanda wasn't safe because of banditry and refugees and that we needed a police escort. We tracked down some men we had met in the bar to ask them how to get safely to Rwanda. The problem, they told us, was that there were refugees in the area, "desperate people, not bad people." The refugee camps in Tanzania housed those who had fled during the Rwanda conflict. Several refugee camps with over a hundred thousand Burundi and Rwanda refugees were located around this area. Despite an agreement signed by Rwanda and Tanzania to repatriate the refugees to Burundi, refugees continued to arrive, and many were still too afraid to return. We heard that one of the issues was that when a refugee camp was full, it could not accept more refugees. So those displaced people had to survive on their own until a spot was available for them in the camp. These were the desperate ones, and bandits preyed on the desperate.

After discussions with the locals, we decided to attempt the trip via the road rather than taking a ferry across Lake Victoria or using a police escort. We would not bush camp but, instead, find a safe place to stay each night.

The road turned out to be a red-dirt track cutting through dense green vegetation. Several hours later, we arrived at the village of Ngara near the Rwanda border and asked for directions to the police station. As we drove into the station, a middle-aged policeman approached our vehicle. We greeted him as we climbed out. I asked where we could camp safely for the night.

"What is your religion?" he asked.

"Presbyterian." I was confused by the question.

"That is not a real religion," he replied.

"What's a real religion?"

"Anglican."

"Oh, yes, that's right. I'm Anglican."

"Good. I will take you to the sisters at the mission—you can camp there. You'll be safe."

The nuns and nurses of an Anglican diocese welcomed us into the hospital grounds. An older woman with a body seemingly made only of bones walked slowly toward me. She reached out to touch my face. I felt her fragile hand brush my cheek as I gazed into her eyes, opaque with cataracts. "*Karibu,*" she whispered—welcome.

We parked on the red gravel beside the grass within the compound. When we got out of the Cruiser, a group of young nuns dressed in blue dresses and white veils giggled and whispered to one another. They could have shouted, and I still wouldn't have understood them, but some spoke English and were interested when I told them I had once worked as a midwife and nurse in South Africa. We talked about their maternity hospital, and they told me about their patients. But when I asked about the refugees they had cared for, they looked away in pain and sadness and struggled to talk about the human tragedy of war.

Tom and I also struggled to make sense of what we'd heard and witnessed. Africa has challenges, but we concluded that, despite the billions of dollars flowing into Africa, foreign aid simply wasn't working. It seemed to be making things worse for the majority of ordinary people. Large international corporations continue to take resources from the continent—minerals, fish, food, oil, and gas—and leave nothing behind. The wealth of Africa is hidden in offshore accounts by corrupt leaders and tax-evading companies. It takes three parties for corruption to work: those willing to pay the bribe, those willing to take the bribe, and those who hide the money. As resources and money fly out, aid agencies and weapons fly in.

I had a restless night, unsure of what to expect going into Rwanda. I had seen the horrific images and read about the brutality of the 1994 Rwanda genocide when the ethnic Hutu majority had slaughtered eight hundred thousand Tutsi minorities in just a hundred days. Twelve years after the genocide, we wondered what had happened to the people at that time. We crossed over the Kagera River at Rusumo Falls the following morning and entered Rwanda. What we saw was not even close to what we'd expected.

Chapter 11
While the World Watched

Rwanda, 2006

I leaned on the railing of the narrow one-way bridge over the dusty-red Kagera River and watched the roaring Rusumo Falls. Dense green vegetation spilled down the steep embankment. In 1994, hundreds of thousands of Rwandese refugees had fled across this bridge, and thousands of bloated corpses had floated beneath it while the world stood back and watched. In silence, Tom and I returned to our Cruiser, where we found a man touching the Canadian flag on our vehicle.

"Canada?" he asked with a broad grin.

"Yes," I replied.

He smiled and asked if we knew Roméo Dallaire. "Very, very good man, very brave," he said. "Canada, you welcome in our country."

As Canadians, we found that people welcomed us throughout the country due to the legacy left behind by the courageous and dedicated humanitarian Roméo Dallaire, a Canadian and the commander of the United Nations peacekeeping mission in Rwanda during the genocide. Risking his life and those of his men, Dallaire and the United Nations peacekeepers saved tens of thousands of lives during the brutal and violent human catastrophe.

We shook hands and thanked the man for his welcome. Once he had gone, we set off for Kigali, the capital of Rwanda, a tiny land-locked country known as the Land of a Thousand Hills. We were surprised to find the road to Kigali in excellent condition and tarred: it had no potholes or litter strewn over it. More people than we were used to seeing walked alongside the road. Neat brick houses perched precariously on the hill ridges. Square patches of land, terraced and cultivated, cut a dramatic swath up the steep hillsides as if a colorful patchwork quilt had been thrown over the country. The color couldn't hide a palpable darkness: the children in the villages were different from other children we had met on our trip. Rwandese children appeared to hold back, just watching us, unsure whether we could be trusted. They didn't run to greet us with happy smiles with hands held out for gifts; instead, they stood quietly, their little arms across their chests, hugging themselves. Youngsters bore scars, others struggled on primitive crutches, and some sat in homemade wheelchairs.

Several hours later, we reached Kigali, a sprawling city spread over several hills, its streets lined with flowering trees, the litter conspicuous by its absence. Motorcyclists wore orange vests; traffic flowed; everything seemed organized and the people disciplined.

Built on a hill overlooking the city, the Kigali Genocide Memorial Centre had opened less than two years before our visit. On arrival, we wondered whether we were in the right place. We were the only ones in the parking lot. Steps down to the garden below led to a large map of the world sculptured into the ground. A flagpole rose from the African continent on the map, and the blue, yellow, and green striped Rwandan flag fluttered in the summer breeze. Bees buzzed among the rose bushes that blossomed in the neat flowerbeds, birds twittered in the trees, and a dog barked in the distance. I breathed in the air, and even the gentle breeze smelled different.

The Kigali Genocide Memorial opened in 2004 on the tenth anniversary of the Rwandan genocide. To assist in establishing the memorial, the Rwandan government requested assistance from the Aegis Trust, an international organization working to prevent genocide. The memorial, therefore, isn't only about Rwanda's genocide; it also includes information about other such horrific crimes throughout the world.

The Polish writer Raphael Lemkin coined the word "genocide" in 1943. The United Nations (UN) currently defines it under international law as a crime, committed when any of the following acts are carried out with the intent to destroy, in whole or in part, a national, ethnical, racial, or religious group:

- killing members of the group
- causing serious bodily or mental harm to members of the group
- deliberately inflicting on the group conditions of life calculated to bring about its physical destruction in whole or in part
- imposing measures intended to prevent births within the group
- forcibly transferring children of the group to another group

I was born shortly after the Nazi Holocaust when the words "never again" were chanted throughout the world. But despite an apparent global commitment to "never again," the world in my lifetime alone has seen the Cambodian genocide under Pol Pot, 1975–1979; the Bosnia-Herzegovina genocide, 1992–1995; and, of course, the Rwandan genocide.

We entered the Kigali Genocide Memorial building to the sounds of our footsteps echoing on the tiled floor. Pegs on a wire strung along the wall held portraits and family photographs of the victims taken before the horror: proud, smiling parents with newborns; toddlers playing and laughing; children in school uniforms and Spider-Man pajamas; lovers holding hands; stern-looking adults and wrinkled, gray-haired grandparents. Ordinary people murdered with primitive weapons—blunt machetes, axes, clubs, knives, and even garden tools. I looked in horror at the weapons used by perpetrators of a genocide the world had watched on TV from the comfort of their living rooms. I, too, had watched the news reports. As I stood on the same ground on which both perpetrators and victims had once stood and breathed the same air they had once breathed, an indescribable terror turned my stomach, and my knees weakened. Never before had I experienced such a profound depth of grief.

At the memorial, we watched video clips from interviews of both survivors and perpetrators. The hacked, tortured, rotting bodies of the victims in the pictures had no voice. What of the voices of the bystanders, the rescuers, and the hunted? No Tutsis escaped the horror, and many moderate Hutus met the same fate.

Two hundred fifty-nine thousand victims currently lay buried at the Kigali Genocide Memorial site. Who were they, what had they seen, and what had they thought of as they were murdered?

Unanswerable questions assailed my consciousness. *How would I have reacted if I had been Tutsi? How hard would I have fought? And if I had been Hutu, would I have risked my life trying to save Tutsis, or would I have believed that the killing of Tutsis was justified?*

"Of course you would have done the right thing," Tom said.

"Nobody can know what they'll actually do until faced with that decision. We're all human. We're all the same." I felt vulnerable, unsure of who I was.

"I know you," Tom insisted; "you would have done the right thing."

"I want to believe that. But how do you explain missionaries and pastors killing the infants they baptized, doctors and nurses murdering the patients they cared for, teachers slaughtering schoolchildren, and professors hacking to death their students?"

Nobody, it seemed, had been immune to the murderous insanity. Just thinking about the mass participation was terrifying.

We left the memorial in silence. I could find no words to describe the brutality of humankind and what we all are capable of doing. I thought of the words of the Polish anthropologist Bronislaw Malinowski: "To judge something, you have to be there." I hadn't been in Rwanda during the genocide, so all I could do was bear witness to the aftermath. I would never understand, but I would remain haunted by the experience nonetheless.

Subdued and thoughtful, Tom and I drove from Kigali to Ruhengeri, located close to Parc National des Volcans. Ruhengeri lies in the Virunga Mountains, a chain of eight mostly dormant volcanoes. Three countries—Uganda, the Democratic Republic of Congo, and Rwanda—share borders in this mountain range. Our guide, Fidel, informed us we would hike up Mount Bisoke in search of the Amahoro mountain gorilla family. For a good reason, the Rwanda Wildlife Conservation places armed game rangers in the mountains to keep a close eye on the gorillas around the clock to protect them from poachers. These rangers would guide Fidel by radio to the gorilla family, which was always on the move.

Fidel used a machete to slash a path through the thick bamboo forest, tall grass, and bushes. With an annual rainfall of eighty inches, the Virunga Mountains' vegetation is dense and the earth muddy. I struggled to keep up, my boots sticking in the glue-like mud. We had no idea how far we would need to hike before seeing the gorillas. Dian Fossey, who wrote *Gorillas in the Mist* and fought to protect the gorillas from poachers, was murdered in these mountains for her efforts. She had witnessed the killing of twenty adult gorillas during the kidnapping of an infant gorilla, later sold to a European zoo. Adult gorillas will and do fight to the death, trying to protect their young. Because human greed, arrogance, and ignorance are pushing and killing gorillas into extinction, I wanted to see one in the wild before the opportunity was gone forever.

Fidel grunted a soft rumble from deep down in his belly to attract the attention of the gorillas. I looked up to see movement in the dense vegetation. The plants swayed, and I heard a rustle, a swish of leaves. I held my breath as a gorilla suddenly moved toward me, her large, warm brown eyes looking directly into mine. Our eyes locked. I was overwhelmed. The exhilaration of being surrounded by fourteen gorillas in the wild was a dream come true.

I listened to the soft grunt of a mother with her infant and watched how tenderly she stroked her baby. She got up to walk, and her infant climbed onto her back for the ride. He turned his head as his mother passed by us, his large brown eyes looking curiously at me. He was so close I could have reached out and touched him.

A giant silverback, twice the size of a man, approached. After making a cautionary study of us, he sat down within feet and ate a celery-like plant. His teeth tore the plant with a crunching sound and, chewing slowly, he watched the youngsters play. They beat their chests as they took flying leaps and tumbled down a slope. Scampering back up, they did it again and again. They played like children on a water-slide in the sun.

I noticed a gorilla hiding behind the bushes, the leaves her only cover. I asked Fidel why that gorilla kept her distance from us and why she stayed away from her family.

"Poachers cut her hand off. She is afraid of you."

His words slammed into me. *To every mountain gorilla, I am their only predator, a human.* Even gorillas know that humans brutalize and kill.

As we began our descent back down the mountain, I felt the rage of hate tear through my core, and I wondered if I could do it—could I kill a poacher to protect a mountain gorilla? If so, was there any rela-tionship between this kind of killing and a murderous ethnic-based genocide? Is violence ever justified, and who is the arbiter of the deci-sion? Rwanda was stripping my emotions naked and raw.

A day later, we arrived at the small town of Gisenyi on the shores of Lake Kivu. Most of the lake lies in the Democratic Republic of Congo, but we were still in Rwanda. It was through Gisenyi that mil-lions of Rwandan refugees had fled across the border to Goma, a town in the Congo.

On the horizon sat the fishermen's boats, sleek and low on the water, their tall fishing rods silhouetted against the azure. Even as the sun set, the world stayed blue, the water rippling against the sky as if one element. We sat on the beach, the air hot and humid, and sipped on a local Mützig beer, a chilled relief.

"Almost every village we passed today had a memorial beside rows of graves," I said, overwhelmed with confusion and sadness. No village had escaped the murders. I continuously struggled to understand what I had witnessed. The United Nations refused to call the Rwanda murders genocide because they weren't sure the massacres met the legal definition. If the massacres had been declared genocide, the UN would have had to intervene. While the Security Council in New York debated the meaning of a word, hundreds of thousands of people were slaughtered. America refused to jam the Rwandan Radio Télévision Libre des Mille Collines's radio waves, which were broadcasting hate and racist propaganda and inciting people to kill. Jamming the radio stations, the Americans said, would "deny the people their freedom of speech." Thousands paid with their lives for that freedom. Unbelievably, expatriates' pets were evacuated while Rwandan children were left behind to be hacked to death. I no longer knew what to think or even to feel. I was numb. I couldn't remember enduring a darker, more hopeless time. The only place of reflection, as always, was the wilderness.

Tucked into the southwest corner of Rwanda and extending south into Burundi is the Nyungwe Forest National Park. The Nyungwe is the largest single tract of montane forest remaining in East and Central Africa and is home to thirteen different primate species, including the chimpanzee. Some of its wildlife has been shot to extinction; there are no more buffalo, and most of its elephants have disappeared in the last thirty years.

The government tourist map indicated that the road from Gisenyi to Gitarama was in good condition and tarred. So, the following morning we headed south through central Rwanda. Soon the nicely tarred road became a dirt road; then the dirt road became a rocky, potholed track; and finally, the rocky trail became a narrow, winding hint of a path. An active military presence remained in the area, so we weren't surprised to see a military Land Cruiser pickup truck heading toward us. Soldiers armed with Belgian FN rifles sat on the back, their feet resting on a footrest made of steel tubing that protruded over the side of the truck. Tom pulled as far as he could to the side of the narrow track to allow them to pass. The engine revving of the military vehicle was broken by the sound of steel grinding against steel. Tom stopped and jumped out of the car to be met by several soldiers waving rifles in his face.

The sergeant stood with his hands on his hips. "This is not my problem," he said.

Tom examined our slightly damaged Cruiser. "No, sir, definitely not. It's the road's fault."

Tom got back in and slammed the door shut. Glancing at me, he said, "You don't argue with a sergeant surrounded by soldiers waving rifles."

We arrived at the Nyungwe Forest National Park late that afternoon as storm clouds busily rearranged themselves overhead. I looked up at the menacing sky, sure that it was going to rain. Traveling independently, we had the advantage of waiting out bad weather, taking a detour, or changing our minds. It was a freedom I treasured and one that I took less and less for granted, having already witnessed so much restriction of that precious commodity.

I lay in bed in the dark, listening to the tropical rain thundering down onto the tin roof of our cabin. I learned that humans and chimpanzees are distant relatives and that we share over 94 percent of our DNA: six million years ago, we shared a common ancestor. I wanted to see and hear chimpanzees in the wild more than ever. The sights and sounds of nature always breathe life and optimism back into my spirit, a rejuvenation I needed more than ever. Nature asks no questions and never judges. I can be exactly who I am—no matter how confused that identity is—without fear of misunderstanding or criticism. And life, in all its various beauty, can be itself too.

The following day, we arranged for trackers to take us down into the valley to search for chimpanzees. Because they live high in the forest canopy, they are difficult to track, and we weren't sure we would see them. The trackers hacked a path through the dense, tangled vegetation with machetes; the hike was strenuous, steep, and slippery. Unable to see my feet, I used a large stick to bushwhack my way down the mountainside. For a forest with over 280 species of birds, it was eerily silent. "Not a good sign," said the tracker. Chimpanzees are located by the sounds of their cries and calls—the vegetation is much too dense for them to be found by sight only—but the silence and the absence of birdsong seemed to swallow up all other sounds. After three hours, a movement stirred in the canopy. I glanced up to see a chimpanzee shifting quietly in the tree above and then disappearing into a canopy of green.

The tracker peered through his binoculars. "The chimps are quiet. They must be hunting for colobus monkeys."

Chimpanzees eat the colobus monkeys, a black-and-white species with a black face trimmed by white fur and a stunning black-and-white fur shawl.

We stopped for a rest, and the trackers went off to find where the troop was heading. When they returned, the news wasn't good.

"There's a troop of colobus monkeys not far away, but the chimps are moving in for a kill, so they won't make noise. The monkeys know the chimps are in the area, so they're hiding high up in the trees, staying still and quiet. We won't be able to find the monkeys or the chimps if they're not making noise."

I lay down, breathless and exhausted, and let the forest floor swallow me up in the silence of the hunt. The stillness of the forest screamed at me, nature's wildness conducting its ancient business in the world above. I waited for the hot, heavy air to be pierced by waves of terrified shrieks of a victim. The desperate cries of the other escaping colobus monkeys and the hunters' howls of a successful kill. But it was not to be. After several hours of unsuccessfully tracking the chimpanzees, we returned to our cabin. The eeriness of a silent forest had been a new experience and one that took many hours to come down from.

The next day we headed to the town of Gikongoro to visit our first genocide-massacre site. Apprehensively, we approached the Murambi Technical School, situated on a hill overlooking the town. An Aegis Trust official quickly approached us in the parking lot to explain that the Murambi Genocide Memorial wasn't yet open to the public. I asked if there was any way we could visit the technical school located behind the memorial. He said he would find someone to show us around and warned us about what we would see.

A few minutes later, a tall, dark, thin man approached. His gray jacket and pants hung on his frame. His walk was slow, as if painful. When he reached us, he welcomed us to the school and introduced himself as Emmanuel, explaining that he was a survivor. He had a soft voice and a gentle handshake, and his gray eyes resembled wet stones pushed deep into his gaunt face. His skin was so tight that it shone in the sunlight, except for the scarred hole above his left eye. The horror of the genocide was visibly and vividly etched into the expression he turned to the world that had hurt and betrayed him.

I lowered my eyes to the ground, unsure if I wanted to hear what happens when humankind turns to uncontrolled evil. We followed him, his shoulders stooped, to the school. During the Rwandan genocide, forty to sixty thousand men, women, and children had crowded into the sixty-four classrooms, spilling out onto the grass around the building.

I entered the classrooms, and the smell of lime and death filled my lungs. I stood in the stillness of one room, hearing the echoes of the screams of terror that had once reverberated off these walls as people were slaughtered. Somehow that eerie silence of the forest came alive to me again, but now as a mass human grief.

Eighteen hundred white lime-encrusted skeletons of the 27,000 exhumed from a mass grave alongside the school were on display in the classrooms. The exhibit is haunting in its simplicity, with the skeletons and shattered bones carefully laid out on the desks and tables. Shreds of a blue dress clung to the skeleton of an unknown woman, and beside her lay a battered toddler with broken bones, an eloquent reminder of what was allowed to happen here. I reached out to touch the cold, hard bones and stroked the child's flattened skull, my fingers tracing the face of a murder victim. I imagined the child's innocent eyes: What had he or she witnessed before the machete fell? I imagined the child's small mouth, wide with horror, and the screams for her or his mother. As a mother myself, a pain ripped through me that I'd never known before. My stomach heaved, and my whole body trembled.

We left the classrooms, and once outside, I heard the sounds of children laughing, shouting, and playing in the village beside the school. Green grass, white clouds above, birds in the sky—the world sounded and looked normal. But it wasn't, not now. Emmanuel told us to follow him.

I stood in the doorway of the school gymnasium and looked in. Rows and rows of clothing hung like washing out to dry on a sunny day. Hundreds of articles of clothing from the exhumed skeletons hung there, a mixture of tattered and blood-stained shirts, dresses, pants, skirts, and children's and infants' clothing. There was no need to speak (I couldn't anyway).

After several minutes, however, Emmanuel eloquently explained the situation. Prior to the genocide, a civil war had raged between the Hutu-dominant government and the opposition party, the Rwanda Patriotic Front (RPF), mainly Tutsis. Emmanuel, a farmer, had lost his job during that time because he was a victim of his birth, a Tutsi. On April 6, 1994, the Rwandan president's plane was shot down, and the Interahamwe—a Hutu paramilitary organization—incited all Hutus to kill all the Tutsis, whom they referred to as *inyenzi*, cockroaches. The Interahamwe and the soldiers set fire to the Tutsis' homes and took their cattle, and the systematic massacres began.

I looked up at Emmanuel and tried to imagine how I would feel, what I would have done if put in such a situation. On April 16, 1994, the mayor of Gikongoro told them to go to the school and that they would be safe there. Emmanuel fled to the apparent sanctuary with his family, along with thousands of other Tutsis. The Interahamwe soon cut off the water supply and denied the Tutsis access to food. The trapped Tutsis became weak but tried to defend themselves by throwing rocks and stones at their attackers. On April 21, the Tutsis were overrun, and forty-five thousand people were murdered, including Emmanuel's family. He paused in silence as if held by the ghosts of his past. "I will stay here, at the school. This is where my family is buried."

We shook hands with Emmanuel, finding only enough words to thank him. Nodding, he turned and walked back up the red dirt road from the parking lot to the school.

Tom didn't want to see any more sites. "That was too hard, much too painful," he said. I replied that I couldn't talk about it yet, so we drove in silence back toward Kigali. The smooth roads, built by the foreign-aid money that poured in after the genocide, made for easy driving. I thought of them as "guilt" roads. They took us past villages where men in pink cotton short-sleeved shirts and shorts—the perpetrator prisoners—worked in the fields or attended the *gacaca*—"justice in the grass"—in the communities.

After the genocide, with the legal system in tatters and the prisons overcrowded with perpetrators, the *gacaca*—a system of justice originating from the traditional system of conflict resolution—was revived to provide justice to both the victims and the detained suspects. Those who participated in the murder of Tutsis and moderate Hutus and who were willing to reveal and apologize for their crimes could have their sentences reduced. Survivors were encouraged to forgive the perpetrators who admitted their crimes.

The road rose over the hills and down into the valleys. Neat, square patches of farms covered the land. We passed more villages, memorials, graveyards, *gacaca* courts, and men in pink. I wanted to visit another memorial site, but Tom refused to stop. He said he couldn't take any more.

"Why do you want to see more?" he said. "What's the matter with you?"

"I don't know. I'm trying to understand what makes a human do this."

"I'll stop, but I'm not going in. I'll wait in the car for you."

At the village of Ntarama, Tom parked under the tree beside the building. A woman was sweeping the path to the door. I got out of the car and walked toward the redbrick church. The woman paused and looked up at me, but she didn't speak or try to stop me in any way. Alone in the church, I stepped over a child's shoe and walked toward the bloodstained wall behind the pulpit. Beneath the wooden pews lay more torn and ripped clothing and shoes. Tiny rays of sun peeped in through the bullet holes in the ceiling.

I stood still, hardly daring to breathe. In the silence, I struggled to understand why the world had allowed this to happen.

I thought of the words of Elie Wiesel: "To remain indifferent is the greatest sin of all."

I had no answers to the world's indifference, which, to my shame, had once included my own. With nothing else to do and nowhere else to go, I returned to the Cruiser with my eyes full of tears.

"You okay?" Tom asked. He reached out and took my hand.

"Yeah," was all I could whisper.

What we witnessed and heard in Rwanda impacted each of us differently. We were both horrified, shocked, and shattered, but what we took to our inner core was different. Tom struggled with the role of the killers—mostly men—in the genocide. I mainly thought about the children in my struggle to know why humans don't do more to protect our most vulnerable.

Chapter 12
On the Shores of Lake Victoria

Uganda, February 2006

We crossed into Uganda on a warm summer day. Only when the temperature climbs above ninety-five degrees do the locals consider it a hot day, and the temperature that day was a pleasant eighty-six degrees. Although the clouds hung low in the sky, rains weren't expected. In Africa, many refer to the seasons as wet or dry seasons, rather than winter or summer. February is the dry season in Uganda. When route planning, we mapped out the wet seasons, planning to avoid the big rains.

At the border, posters of the Uganda president with the words VOTE NRM YOWERI K MUSEVENI were plastered on billboards. Uganda's first multiple-party election in twenty years was about to happen.

That evening, we set up camp on the grassy shore of Lake Bunyonyi. The word "Bunyonyi" means "place of many little birds." Fishermen and other boatmen glided silently on the glassy lake in dugout canoes, delivering goods and people to the many islands and villages. In the distance, I heard children laughing and singing, their voices soothing, almost hypnotic. Sitting in the shade of a large eucalyptus tree, filled with hundreds of small, noisy, black-face yellow weavers and scruffy gray-and-white Levaillant's cuckoos, I felt my whole being, weary from tension, relax.

Meanwhile, Tom wandered off and met a young man, Isaac, who offered to teach Tom how to cook crayfish caught from the lake. Together they left for the market and returned with a small bag of freshly captured crayfish, tomatoes, onions, green peppers, and spices. They peeled, cut, and chopped the ingredients, tossed them into a frying pan, and, over a beer, shared their stories. Aromas from our simmering dinner wafted through the air.

The warm evening breeze tossed the few low-lying clouds above. I wandered off but hadn't gone far before I sat down on the grass beneath towering Tugu palm trees, which some locals believe were planted by elephants. As I watched a bright blue kingfisher bird swoop low over the water, thousands of thoughts and images of our travels flashed through my mind like a movie on fast-forward. I thought of the people I had met and the humanity in the stories they had shared. I thought about my story of emptiness and unfulfillment, which I now realized was so insignificant in the face of what I had experienced and witnessed. A splash of water attracted my attention, and I turned to see the kingfisher emerge from the lake with a tiny fish held tightly in its long beak. Stirred by the motion, I got up and returned to our campsite. Tom had set the table, and Isaac was dishing up three plates of a steaming crayfish stew, small bananas, and freshly baked bread.

Uganda spans the southern and northern hemispheres, and we crossed the equator the following day. A large concrete circle with UGANDA EQUATOR written on top marked the equator's precise location. We laughed, posing for photographs with a foot in each hemisphere, and recorded another milestone in our journey. Tom reminded me that the water goes down the drain clockwise in the southern hemisphere and counterclockwise in the northern hemisphere, a phenomenon known as the Coriolis effect.

Kampala, the capital and the largest city in Uganda, is a modern, bustling, noisy urban environment with shopping malls, golf courses, and high-rise apartments, all intermingled with the more traditional stalls, wandering goats, and litter-strewn streets. There were few street signs, and only two traffic lights appeared to be working. Market stalls and people chatting loudly above the traffic noise spilled over the sidewalks and into the streets. We had difficulty understanding how such cities functioned; traffic flowed without any apparent direction from any official. Everybody sensed the next action and who should take it as if guided by some invisible force. Bewildered, we simply went with the flow until we were spat out on the other side of the city.

Eventually, we drove up a road and turned into the Red Chilli Hideaway. The receptionist greeted us, but I sensed something wasn't right. She spoke to others and, waving her hand, directed us to where we could camp as if speeding us out of the office. Staff glanced in our direction and whispered to one another. Later we learned that the Lord's Resistance Army (LRA), led by Joseph Kony, had murdered the campsite owner at Murchison Falls in northern Uganda three months earlier.

The mood at Red Chilli was one of dismay and anger, a feeling I couldn't reenter so soon after Rwanda. Aching with despair at humans' capacity for brutality, I simply had no strength left to deal with another senseless death. Exhausted from witnessing people on the edge of survival and the blatant disregard for human rights and the rights of other species, I lay down on our bed. Despair washed over me. I closed my eyes to shut out the world.

We set out the following morning to get our Cruiser serviced. The young auto mechanics at the garage chatted to us about the upcoming election, explaining that they were getting their passports ready because they were expecting trouble. The country was restless. I felt a heightened sense of alertness for potential challenges.

Later, Tom and I went to the Uganda Wildlife Education Centre (UWEC) on Lake Victoria's shore. UWEC was a sanctuary for abandoned and injured animals, and the director introduced himself and arranged for his "best guide," Jimmy, to take us to meet the rescued wildlife.

Jimmy, a student, shorter and slimmer than Tom and at least thirty years younger, had a smile as huge as his passion for animals.

He introduced us to the chimpanzees in his care. He discussed their unique personalities: who loved to tease and play, who was serious, who was the leader, and who was the clown of the troop. I leaned on the fence and watched a small young chimpanzee using a stick as a tool to try to get some leaves out of the water. Two young white rhinos followed Jimmy, who had a bucket of food, like excited, lumbering puppies.

A large gray shoebill bird, so called because of its shoehorn-shaped bill, stood silently and watched Jimmy approach him as if an old friend had come to visit. A lone, shy De Brazza's monkey watched us from the tree branches above while a keeper in a field held out some leafy forage as a nervous but hungry giant forest hog slowly approached. I held my breath. Would he trust the man with the food? Jimmy explained that the forest hog had just been rescued and that they were trying to teach him to trust people.

"It takes a long time, you need much patience, but we do it," he said.

Big Mama, a Nile crocodile, rested on the banks of a pond with her mouth wide open. Lake flies in the thousands hovered in the air, and a red-tailed monkey named Nakabugo swung between the branches of a drum tree.

"Let me take you to meet Furaha," Jimmy said. "She's still in isolation."

Furaha, a tiny young, orphaned chimpanzee, had just arrived at the facility. She huddled alone in the corner of a green metal cage. As tenderly as possible, I reached out and wrapped my fingers around one of the cage's cold bars.

"Come," I whispered so softly that I hardly heard myself speak. Furaha turned and looked at me, her scared eyes penetrating my whole being. I waited. "Come," I finally repeated. Furaha moved cautiously toward me. When she was close enough, I put my finger through the bars and stroked her soft black hair. The young chimp reached out, placed her tiny fingers on my hand, and gently petted me. Then she extended her little arm beyond the bars and tenderly stroked my arm. She pulled back her hand and took mine, and, for a moment, we held hands and made eye contact. Though separated by six million years of evolution, both humans and chimpanzees require care and tenderness to survive. I wanted to hold Furaha to reassure her that she was safe. I thought of Jane Goodall's 1971 book, *In the Shadow of Man*, a signed first edition Tom had given me as a wedding gift. Now, in as direct a way as possible, I understood Jane's passion and dedication to the chimpanzees and why she had asked the question "What if a chimpanzee wept tears when he heard Bach thundering from a cathedral organ?" I knew that little Furaha must have wept when alone and lost.

Shaking Jimmy's hand and thanking him, I struggled to find the words to describe my feelings. It was a roller-coaster day of emotions for me, inspired by Jimmy and his passion and crushed by the bewilderment I saw in the little chimp's eyes.

After the intensity of the previous few weeks, we decided to spend a few days relaxing at Jinja on the shore of Lake Victoria. The White Nile flows out of Lake Victoria and begins its 4,000-mile journey to the Mediterranean Sea—our final destination. We planned to go via Lake Tana in Ethiopia, where the Blue Nile begins its journey north to the Mediterranean. The Blue and White Nile converge into the single mighty Nile in Sudan. One of the world's great and most storied rivers, the Nile spurred bitter rivalries in the early twentieth century among several British explorers: Burton, Speke, and Livingstone. They spent most of their lives trying to be the first to discover the river's source. Our ambition was much more modest, and yet the Nile fever was definitely palpable.

From our campsite, we watched a bloodred sunset over the river. Apparently, it takes three months for one drop of water to make the journey from here to the Mediterranean—about the same time we estimated it would take us to get there. I experienced a full range of emotions as the realization slowly sank in of just how far we had traveled, how far we still had to go, and how different the northern part of our trip might be as we followed the Nile's legendary course.

My journey was like the flow of the river. Each day, I meandered into the unknown and discovered a new part of me. At times, I found strength and pride; at other times, I encountered only weakness and shame. My freedom in the wilderness and new cultures had begun to shape a new identity. Africa had defined me as a child and was defining me once more.

Tom stoked the embers of our campfire, and glowing sparks escaped into the evening air. I held my mug of coffee, blowing the steam from my cup into the swirling smoke as I glanced at Tom. When we left Calgary, I hadn't cared much if we even stayed together. But now, the possibility of reclaiming our relationship stirred in me.

I watched the river crash over boulders, slice branches off trees, toss dugouts with abandon, thrash the rocks with its power, and then gently glide until it tumbled over the edge of the world, foaming up white with rage. Birds watched from above as fish were tossed about below; even crocodiles and hippos knew to avoid this river section. I reached out to touch Tom's arm. "I couldn't have done it without you," I said.

I loved the energy I had back in my life. During the times I'd felt empty, I was indifferent to whether I lived or died. There were also times I'd wanted to die. But now, I wanted my life back in full. I had lived for too long in one dimension: the pursuit of happiness and contentment that had led only to emptiness. I wanted to be unafraid to venture off the grid, to test myself, to be flexible and adaptable. Ultimately, there is no such thing as permanent self-fulfillment or happiness; they are just fleeting moments in our lives. I needed to know both my strengths and my weaknesses, both my genius and my stupidity. I needed to know all of me. Then and only then could I begin to know Tom and others.

As if reading my thoughts, Tom suddenly squeezed my hand. "You're stronger and tougher than I ever imagined," he said.

A rustle in the grass caught my attention, and I looked up to see two young men standing nearby. They smiled and introduced themselves, and we invited them to join us although, I explained, we had only two mugs, so we couldn't offer them anything to drink.

"No problem," said the youngest, introducing himself as Austin. A cigarette dangled from his mouth, and he kicked at the sand with his bare feet.

He announced that he and his companion, James, were river guides. He asked us if we had considered going on a white-water rafting adventure on the river. "It's intense," he said.

"It's grade five plus rapids," added James. "Guaranteed to flip you, and you'll taste the river."

This class of rapid—violent rapids; raging turbulence; large, unavoidable waves; and considerable drops—typically requires expert white water rafting skills.

I glanced at Tom, wondering what he was thinking. We both knew that the largest commercially rafted hydraulic hole (which can suck you down) was part of this river run, but we had avoided discussing whether to raft the river or not.

Tom thanked the young men for their offer but told them we didn't want to do it. Disappointed, the two guides walked back into the shadows.

The last white water Tom and I had experienced happened during a two-week canoe trip down the Nahanni River in Canada, which ended in a life-or-death struggle. Capsized in huge rapids, we'd been swept down the raging river through a canyon for nearly four miles in thirty-nine-degree water. I was rescued from the river unconscious and with severe hypothermia.

Shaking off the memory, I turned, looked directly at Tom, took a deep breath, and told him, "I want to do it."

"I don't want to go through that again," he said and looked away.

The tense silence between us was broken only by the roar of the wild river below. After the Nahanni incident, Tom had told me how petrified he'd been when he thought I was dead.

I closed my eyes and remembered being tossed beneath icy waves. Kicking hard, I followed the bubbles to the surface. Freezing waters gripped me with millions of painful stings. I grabbed a rope on our upside-down canoe. "Hang on," Tom had yelled. We clung to our overturned canoe as waves pushed us down beneath the glacier-fed water and smashed us against rocks. After four miles, we finally exited the canyon. I was exhausted, and my body numb. As the river swept us toward the next canyon, I told Tom I couldn't hang on. I believed I was going to die, but a few minutes later, we were rescued by two fellow canoeists. Wasting no time, they didn't pull me up onto their canoe but quickly tied me to its side so I wouldn't slip underwater. Tom swam, and Brechin and Bruce paddled powerfully toward the shore.

In that river, I survived more than just my imminent death; the Nahanni also gave me back my life. Once rescued, I was exuberantly grateful to be alive. But the banality and emptiness of western suburban life, combined with my doubts and uncertainties, kept me from being able to sustain that gratitude.

Now, on the banks of the Nile, I looked up at the African sky of stars and again felt a sense of wonder and gratitude at being alive. But this time, I vowed not to sacrifice those sensations for mere comfort and security.

"Tom, I know you're concerned, but I've got to do this. I'm ready to get back in the rapids."

As with life itself, I would never know a river standing on the banks; I would only know the river when tossed about in its flow.

"And I want you to come with me," I said, reaching out to touch Tom's arm. "I would like us to do this together."

We both knew expert kayakers would be following the raft, ready to rescue anyone in trouble, and that the water was much warmer than the water of the Nahanni.

Tom stood and tossed a stick into our campfire. He remained quiet for a few minutes before turning to me. "I'll think about it. I'll see how I feel in the morning," he said, then he walked away.

I stayed at the campfire, concerned with his hesitancy but also surprised at my need to raft the river. For our relationship to survive, there had to be more give and take; we both had to sacrifice some of our desires, needs, and wants. When I decided to walk away from our comfortable but empty life in Calgary, I'd thought only of myself. But now I heard the words of the woman in the coffin, who had whispered to me, "Treasure your relationships." I couldn't have it all my way. If Tom was unwilling to join me on the river raft, I would not go. I returned to our campsite.

Tom was sitting on a rock beside the Cruiser, the flame of a small candle flickering in the dark. I leaned down over his body, which smelled of campfire and sweat. He sipped on a bottle of beer. "What're you thinking?" I asked.

He shook his head slowly, his chin resting on his left fist, and replied, "Why do you always want to do such damn risky things?" He tightened his fist around the neck of the bottle of beer, that same clenched fist that had held me tightly in the Nahanni, refusing to let go.

I kicked off my shoes and sat down on the damp grass. I listened to the shrieks of bats as they flew above me. I thought of the dark abyss of my mind when I'd decided to walk out of my life. My thoughts had screamed at me, but in the end, I had listened to the quiet, still voice of my heart telling me to let go, to surrender, and to not be afraid to walk into the unknown.

"Tom." I hesitated, stuck for words. "Are you afraid something might happen to me on the river?"

He didn't look at me. "No," he said. He relaxed his shoulders and looked up. "If you want to raft this river, I'll come."

The following morning, we registered with four other travelers for the eighteen-mile trip. Full of nervous anticipation, I stepped into the raft. The guide explained how to navigate the three sets of rapids, Silverback, Dead Dutchman, and the Bad Place. Before we set off, we practiced flipping and pulling ourselves back into the large red inflatable rubber raft.

Before long, the gentle waters turned into a bucking, churning mass of bubbling power as we plunged over the Bujagali Falls. The raft bounced around, and bodies flew into one another, tossed about at the mercy of the wild water and huge waves. We cheered as we regained our breath and realized we were still in the raft. Soon, however, as we approached another class 5 rapid, the unforgiving river suddenly tossed us into the water. After a dozen harrowing seconds, we all clambered back into the raft and then drifted and paddled slowly downstream. More rapids frothed and foamed in our path. Finally exhausted, I could no longer pull myself back into the raft after each spill and needed help to get back in.

Eventually, we arrived at the Bad Place, the notorious class 6 rapid guaranteed to take you on the "white water ride of your life." The guides said it was optional, and only those who chose to brave the Bad Place should do so. Tom, a powerful swimmer, decided to go along for the ride. The raging river's roar brought back memories of the Nahanni, so I decided to watch from the shore.

It happened quickly: A colossal hole sucked the raft down until it abruptly stopped in the vertical position. Tom found himself upside down underwater with someone on top of him. Unable to move, he let the river turn him around three or four times before he could orient himself.

He emerged from the water, grinning. "Wow! That *is* a bad place."

Once on the shore, those who had tackled the Bad Place sat in stunned silence. The local kayakers and rafting guides chatted away as if it had just been another day at the office. We shared a few beers and talked about local politics. Like the mechanic in Kampala, they expressed concern about the upcoming election in less than four weeks. Tom and I decided we would leave Uganda before the elections. We didn't want to risk a complicated struggle to leave a foreign country in crisis.

On January 30, 2006, we headed to the Uganda-Kenya border at Malaba. By now, I considered us to be border-crossing experts. We knew the ropes and believed we would be through and into Kenya in no time. But approaching the Malaba border crossing, we noticed a line of trucks parked alongside the road for several miles. We drove off the road across the fields, passing all the trucks, but once at the actual border crossing, we realized we were going nowhere. More trucks completely blocked all access to it. Police and military personnel were everywhere. And the tension was high as men yelled at one another.

A military official approached us and shouted, "Border closed! Three days." He waved us away. "Go back! You can't get through." He refused to tell us why.

His aggressive manner concerned us. Unnerved by not knowing what was going on, we decided to head to Busia, another Uganda-Kenya border crossing. But several hours later, we arrived at a similar scene, trucks blocking the Busia crossing. Military personnel refused to allow us to enter the border-crossing enclosure.

In frustration, we parked the Cruiser behind the long line of trucks and walked to the border crossing. Truckers sat in the shade of their vehicles, eating, drinking, smoking, and talking loudly, while others slept on cardboard sheets beneath their trucks. At the border, a man approached and said he would help us cross into Kenya. Tom thanked him but said we would try on our own first. We walked to a brick building with a sign over the door that read IMMIGRATION.

Without a word, an immigration officer took our passports and stamped us out of Uganda. He nodded in the direction of customs.

"The border's blocked. You can't go," the customs official said.

His refusal presented a problem because we had to complete all the required documentation before finding a way out of the country. With our passports stamped, we could leave, but to take our vehicle out, we needed our official carnet document to be stamped.

Tom looked around for the man who had offered to help us. "Let's see if we can find that fellow."

"We'll be in trouble if we can't get the Cruiser out," I said. I felt a knot in my stomach.

Eventually, we found the man. He introduced himself as Dembe and said he could assist us. He explained that a Kenyan truck driver had been involved in an accident with a military convoy, and three Ugandan soldiers were killed. The Kenyan driver, taken to the police station, had "mysteriously died" there. The outraged truckers had now blocked all the Uganda-Kenya border crossings, demanding an explanation and the release of the trucker's body. The crowd's anger was at the boiling point.

As the border blockade had nothing to do with the upcoming election, I felt a sense of relief. At least we could technically leave Uganda despite the military telling us the border was closed.

"We still need to find a way to get into Kenya," Tom said.

I nodded. I suggested Tom focus on getting the Cruiser stamped out of Uganda. "And I'll walk to Kenyan immigration and get our passports stamped into Kenya," I said.

With our passports, I set off to walk across no-man's-land to Kenya. Once I arrived, I entered the immigration office and handed the border official our two passports.

"Where is the other party?" the young officer inquired while waving flies away.

"He's too busy to come."

The officer pulled the passports toward him and slowly flicked through all the pages. "You go far." He looked up. "You been Kenya before?"

"Yes, beautiful country," I said.

He found a clean page and stamped both passports. I could hardly believe how smoothly the process had gone. Almost giddy, I walked back to Uganda.

Tom sat waiting in the shade of a tree. "The man with the carnet stamp's coming later." Tom turned to me, grinned, and said, "He's at lunch now, and then he still needs to have a nap."

I sighed. "Well, at least we have our passports sorted out." We were officially stamped out of Uganda and into Kenya but still trapped in the former.

With newfound patience, we sat and watched events unfold between the police, the military, and the truckers. The situation was tense and the crowd restless. When the man with the stamp arrived, Tom showed him how to complete the vehicle carnet. We returned to the Uganda customs office, and after significant haggling, the Uganda customs official handed us a grubby scrap of paper with a handwritten number on it. But we were still in Uganda with no apparent way out. Truckers watched us with interest but made no attempt to move their trucks to allow us to pass.

Dembe waved his arm. "Come, I show you how to get to Kenya."

Together with Dembe, we returned to our Cruiser, which we had parked behind the trucks, and we headed back the way we'd come. After several miles, we turned off the road. We drove across a field, past stalls, mud houses, people, trees, and fields of cassava and Acholi long-horned cattle, avoiding all police and military.

"Stop," said Dembe. He got out of the Cruiser and pointed to a tiny opening, a stone stairway between two buildings. "You go through there. You be in Kenya."

He said he couldn't come any farther with us. We thanked him and said farewell. As I watched him disappear, I wondered uneasily, *Exactly where are we?* As the driver, I faced a steep, narrow stairway between two buildings: not a road, just a simple pedestrian stairway passage. I thought about it for a moment. "I'll never squeeze through there," I said.

Tom got out. "I'll pull in the side mirrors and direct you."

I positioned the Cruiser in line with the staircase, then, with inches to spare and holding my breath, I bounced the Cruiser down the stairway. Every stair seemed to be a cliff edge I was driving over.

When I was finally through the passage, I emerged onto an open field. I leaned out of the window and turned to Tom. "Do you think we're actually in Kenya?" I asked.

"We'll find out once we find a road." Tom got back into the car. We knew our latitude and longitude, so we were not lost in the world, just lost on the map.

We drove across a field heading south until we came to a dirt track, onto which I turned. After a while, several men in uniforms waved us down.

Tom took off his sunglasses. "They're Kenyan police, so we must be in Kenya." He rolled down the window and greeted the officials.

After questioning us, they examined our passports and the scrap of paper issued by the Uganda customs, and they waved us past. Eventually, we joined up with the main road. We turned south for Kisumu, a port city located on the east shore of Lake Victoria.

We slept at Lake Nakuru in an unfenced campsite, under the moonlight, listening to the sounds of a night that never sleeps. Early the next morning, we stood on the lakeshore, the warm, wet mud oozing over my sandals, and watched a flurry of activity in the sky. On the land and in the water, millions of pink flamingos and thousands of pelicans and marabou storks stirred up the smells of wet feathers, fish, and bird poop all around us. I marveled at the flock of thousands of flamingos, a shifting and shimmering cloud of pink and white across the cloudless blue sky, and I smiled at their cries, which sounded like squeaky duck calls. Meanwhile, the pelicans ruffled their white feathers and beat the brown water with their wings. As always, the mysteries of nature filled me with awe.

We returned to our Cruiser and began the search again for more wildlife. We immediately spotted a black rhino in the bush; he seemed agitated, spraying the trees and marking his territory. He turned and looked at us menacingly, his agitation growing. The dust whirled around as he headed in our direction.

Tom wondered if we should move the Cruiser. "No way," I said. "Sit tight and watch."

The rhino gathered speed. Fresh blood ran from large gashes on his side and under his head.

With my adrenaline on high alert, I held up my camera and clicked. "He's enraged. He's wounded—he must have been in a territorial fight with another rhino."

A rhino weighs about one ton and can easily roll most vehicles if it hits them hard enough. The massive animal rumbled closer. I could smell the dust kicked up and the blood on his hide. His actions startled the birds out of the trees. Tom started the engine. The rhino slowed to a trot and then stood still just a few feet away, his whole manner hostile. We did not move. After a minute, the rhino walked up to the vehicle and crossed the road directly in front of us.

"He's awesome," I said in a hushed voice.

Rhinos are spectacular giants but are critically endangered. They are slaughtered for their horns, which are exported to Asian markets and sold as cures for certain diseases, as virility enhancers, or simply as status symbols for the rich. Experts estimate that African rhinos will soon be extinct. I felt numbing despair at this senseless slaughter of wildlife.

A few days later, we drove into Nairobi, Kenya's capital, and headed to a campsite. On our first night, humongous rats attacked us. The menacing rodents spent the entire night scrambling all over our Cruiser, both inside and outside, knocking objects over and continuously setting off the car alarm as we tried to sleep in our roof-top tent. They built nests in our engine, ate their way into the car, chewed through our containers, and generally made themselves at home. After a disturbing night, we cleaned the Cruiser, threw away the food, put anything we could in the fridge, and hoped for the best. The second night, however, the rats returned with all their friends and set off the car alarm again. Tom leaped from the tent, and a monstrous rat jumped out of a container and right onto his chest.

"We need metal containers," he lamented.

"These rats would bring can openers."

Tom sighed. "I'm concerned they'll chew through the hydraulic pipes or the electrical wiring."

After days of battling rats in Nairobi, we decided to leave and head to Ethiopia through northern Kenya. However, the owner of the camp where we were staying warned us that "the Isiolo-Moyale road is currently reported to be the most dangerous in Africa." He advised us to drive in convoys with other travelers or with security. The distance was only three hundred miles, but it was a dusty, potholed, bone-jar-ringly corrugated road. It would take at least two long days of driving through an area well-known for bandits, sporadic violent conflicts between tribes, and desperate refugees crossing in from Somalia and Sudan. There was a food shortage and a drought; cattle were dying. A couple trying to make the trip in a day had rolled their vehicle.

"You must go slow. You can't try to do it in a day," the owner of the camp warned us.

Unfortunately, no other travelers were planning to head to Ethiopia. After discussing our options and weighing the risks, I wanted to proceed, but Tom was reluctant. As seemed to be the case so often, we had a difficult decision to negotiate, one that, yet again, lay bare the essential differences between us.

I left Tom at our campsite and headed to the communal room where travelers sat around chatting, plotting routes on maps, exchanging useful GPS coordinates, or catching up on email. I sat on an old kitchen chair, leaned forward, and rested my elbows on my knees. Several bugs circled the yellow light bulb. The room smelled of sweat, cigarette smoke, and stale beer.

I felt confused and conflicted, thinking that perhaps Tom was right: we shouldn't take any more risks. And yet Africa was compelling me forward, almost against my will, or at least my conscious will. Caught in the continent's powerful flow, I wanted to continue heading north.

Chapter 13

The Most Dangerous Road

Kenya, February 2006

I woke unsettled before the sun rose. The previous day, Tom and I had been unable to agree on whether to take the notorious Isiolo-Moyale road, which the camp owner had warned us about. Uncertainty and a nagging sense that our relationship's newfound amity still contained too much discord made sleep difficult. But regardless, we needed to make decisions.

The Isiolo village is the gateway to northern Kenya, a rugged and desolate wilderness where life had changed little over the decades. Isiolo is also the start of the only road heading north to the only official border crossing into Ethiopia. We had no option; if we wanted to continue to Cairo, we had to drive this road. Tom was hesitant because of the safety concerns voiced by those at the campsite.

I lay in bed and listened to the hum of Nairobi stirring. I thought of all we had seen and done and all the risks we had taken to get this far. We had different fears and concerns. I was fearful of something happening to Tom and afraid of not being able to cope on my own. Tom feared not being able to protect us if we ran into trouble. He would get angry with me when I argued with officials. "I'm the one who's going to be in the fight if things get out of hand. Not you," he would say.

But we had agreed on one key point. If one of us felt unsafe, we would not proceed. Safety, in this instance, meant waiting for a military convoy to accompany us, but that could take weeks. In the meantime, the cat-sized rats presented another serious risk by gradually destroying our vehicle. We needed to get moving.

Our breakfast was the usual bowl of oats and a cup of coffee, which we enjoyed quietly amid the familiar haste of others. In the bustling, noisy campground, some travelers were packing up, while others were route planning, fixing vehicles, catching up with washing, restocking their supplies, or sharing travel tales. Our silence, by comparison, was deafening.

We met several people driving the Cape-to-Cairo route. All were young and childless, taking a career gap year before settling down or having children. We were older and had known Africa before they were even born.

Several at the camp had driven south from Ethiopia to Nairobi and heard that we were debating about driving the road north. They shared their experiences and gave us their opinions. Others who had decided against going the Isiolo-Moyale stood around and listened. Arguments, thoughts, questions, and heated discussions flew about. Most who had driven the road were waiting for car parts to replace those that had been cracked or destroyed on the road.

"The corrugations are horrendous. One of our shock absorbers needed replacing, and we got three punctures."

"We only had one puncture. But we had to replace our shock absorbers, and our suspension cracked."

"There was a bandit attack two weeks ago. I didn't ride my motorbike; I hitched a ride on a truck. That road's bloody dangerous."

"Don't bother going in a convoy. Everyone goes at a different speed—it's useless."

"Don't go alone. Go in a convoy. It's too unsafe."

"Trust me, that road will wreck your car."

Tom got up from the table to do the breakfast dishes, and the crowd wandered off.

"I'm concerned about our security," he said. "Everyone's telling us it's the most dangerous road in Africa right now."

We confirmed that the Kenyan government had put security measures in place but could not determine precisely what these measures involved. It was difficult to decide whether or not the stories we'd heard were gross exaggerations.

"We could go via Lake Turkana," I said. "It's supposed to be a more scenic drive." We'd heard reports of travelers who felt that the Isiolo-Moyale road was too risky even with a convoy. They had chosen to go via Lake Turkana, despite the lack of an official border crossing. Although that road was also challenging, it was reported to be safer.

Tom shook his head. "No. That track gets you into Ethiopia, but there's no official border there. It's far too risky crossing anywhere but at an official border crossing."

Ethiopia was known to be particular about paperwork, and rumors abounded concerning a couple arrested after entering the country without proper documentation.

"You're right. So why don't we at least go to Isiolo? The convoys leave from there, and we can get updated information from the locals about the road and security risks."

Thirty minutes later, we were fighting Nairobi's morning traffic on our way north to Isiolo. Despite our concerns, the challenges of traveling through uncharted territories always energized and invigorated me. I knew we would get to Ethiopia—I just didn't know then that we would face a tragic and challenging life-changing experience there.

While en route to Isiolo, we decided to treat ourselves to a special lunch in Nanyuki at the Trout Tree restaurant, located on the banks of the Burguet River near Mount Kenya. Built like a tree house in a Mugumo fig tree, the restaurant serves expensive wines, gourmet cheeses, and trout freshly caught from the pond below. After nearly five months of camping, the prospect seemed decadent.

British military soldiers in training packed the restaurant, but we looked more battle weary than they did. Tom hadn't shaved since leaving Canada. His disheveled beard matched his unruly head of hair. My body had discarded the fat it didn't need, and my muscles had come alive with power and strength. We were healthier, stronger, and fitter than we'd been in years. Our bodies and minds thrived in our new lifestyle; simple eating, increased physical activity, heated debates, and discoveries made a powerful health tonic. With every sense on high alert all day, I collapsed exhausted into a deep, long sleep each night.

"You'd better enjoy this meal," Tom said. "You could be eating and wearing dust for the next few days."

Later that afternoon, we arrived in Isiolo, a small frontier town and the end of the tarred road. We located a lodge west of Isiolo run by a Dutch couple, who allowed us to camp on their property. After supper, we shared our concerns about the road with them. They confirmed that the road was notoriously unsafe and recommended that people travel in convoys with armed soldiers. However, there was no reliable information about when the next convoy would leave. Likely sensing our impatience, they quickly added that there had recently been a deadly attack but that the perpetrators had been captured.

"So you should be okay to go now," the husband concluded. In an odd way, we found this final bit of information somewhat reassuring.

That night, I lay in bed in the dark, listening to the sounds of crickets and other critters screaming at one another.

"Maybe we should go right away," I whispered. "We could leave early in the morning."

Tom turned on his flashlight. "Perhaps you're right. They did say we should be okay to go."

My heart lurched with the anticipation of heading north. "Yeah, the sooner we leave, the better."

We discussed what we needed to do to minimize the risks. To make it to Marsabit, an outpost-trading center, on the first day, we would drive slowly. We'd fill the auxiliary fuel tank before we left because there was no guarantee we'd be able to refuel en route. Tom thought our Kevlar tires would be fine on the volcanic rock around

Marsabit. Regardless, I knew we had twenty-four grueling hours of driving and nothing more than dust, potholes, and corrugations ahead. Never in my life had I wished for two days of boredom. I had always said I would die of it, but right then, boredom was precisely what would keep us alive.

Before we left, the lodge owner gave us his phone number and said to call him if we ran into trouble. "And whatever you do, don't stop for anyone. It could be an ambush."

The boom across the road was up; the tarred road ended, and the potholed, bone-rattling, corrugated gravel section began. We estimated it would take us twelve hours to get to Marsabit.

Shortly after we left Isiolo, we arrived at our first roadblock manned by armed soldiers. They questioned us, checked our documents, and then waved us through. We passed several more soldiers standing on the roadside and were stopped at a few more roadblocks. After about an hour, there were no more roadblocks or soldiers, and there was almost no traffic.

We entered a world unlike any I'd ever experienced. Men guided camel caravans heavily laden with packs. Women collected water from drying streams, and dried-out carcasses of dead cattle lay twisted on the parched earth. After three hours, we stopped to change drivers. The dust and heat penetrated every one of my pores, and the earth screamed for water below a cloudless sky. I gulped down the warm water from my bottle. Two small children burdened with bundles of goods on their heads walked past us, the air wafting off them filled with the smell of dust, sweat, and tears.

The dusty road seemed endless. To pass the time, we talked and reminisced. We struggled to make sense of what we had witnessed throughout our journey. Surely, we said, every person deserves the fundamental right to a decent life. We agreed that our journey would be empty without the things that enriched our lives and the world's different cultures, languages, customs, traditions, and beliefs. I imagined that with globalization, every person would eventually be reduced to a single monotone consumer, wearing the same clothing, eating the same food, uttering the same words, and dancing to the same beat of the music. A world robbed of diversity would be as if rainbows one day become just one color—gray. Perhaps even the birds would sing only one song.

The large-scale destruction of nature and the disappearance of wildlife we had seen gutted us. We already knew that humans' desire for more material wealth than is required to live was happening at the expense of the planet, especially in the western world. We were gobbling up all the earth's resources as fast as we could. But life in the first world insulated us from the worst of the catastrophe. For many, visiting developing countries would be eye-opening, and it would be hard for those eyes not to be filled with tears. I felt more frightened for future generations than I ever had. *What will the planet that we leave them be like? Denuded of other species, of natural resources, of cultural diversity, will the earth even be recognizable?*

Tom and I discussed our lives and how we had lived prior to coming on this trip. In Calgary, we thought we needed everything we had, but we certainly had a great deal more than we needed. Now we lived with so little, did more with less, and our lives felt fuller and richer. We agreed that we would strive for a more sustainable lifestyle when we returned home.

We were also working better together. "Yep," said Tom, "we never would have gotten through the Uganda-Kenya border at the beginning of the trip."

"I agree. I would never have walked across no-man's-land to get our passports stamped." I chuckled. "It would never have crossed my mind to do that."

"Getting across that border took teamwork," he said.

Near the end of a long day, we saw ahead a car stopped alongside the road, facing toward us. Several men in the middle of the road waved at us to stop. The car engine hood was open. We glanced at each other, unsure whether we should stop or hit the gas pedal. Could this be an ambush setup? The kind we'd been warned about? The men didn't look menacing or appear to have any weapons. We were in a desert, the temperature unbearably hot, with no water in sight.

Tom stared ahead. I heard the tension in his voice. "Perhaps they just need some help."

I slowed down as I approached the men. My sweaty hands clenched the steering wheel. "What do you think? Should I stop?"

"Yeah. Stop."

Tentatively I applied the brakes. We came to a halt, and a man rushed toward us, shouting something we couldn't understand. Tom rolled down his window as we drew up alongside their car. He leaned out and said, "English."

"Push, push." The man waved his arms to indicate they wanted us to push their car.

Tom paused, then opened the car door and got out. The men and Tom leaned over the engine, inspecting it. Then Tom turned to me and said, "They'll need a miracle to get this car moving again. It looks as if it's going to fall apart at any moment."

A middle-aged man reached into the battered car and pulled out a new set of points. He replaced the old ones, and Tom told me to "gently push their car from behind" with our Cruiser, which I did. But their engine remained dead. The man removed the points, threw them away, and got another set of points, which he inserted into the distributor. I pushed their car from behind again several times before the struggling engine spluttered to life. Wild cheers of joy burst from the men and Tom. The driver emerged from the car, his whole face smiling, and, with his hands held together in prayer, he bowed his head and thanked us. I watched the men, chatting and laughing, climb back into their car. They turned, waved, and continued south on their way.

Tom returned to the Cruiser. "We did the right thing," he said.

I nodded, knowing that we'd just received another lesson. We had to be able to assess situations quickly and decide whether we were facing a holdup, a regular roadblock, or just someone needing help.

We arrived safely at Marsabit, where many refugees from war-torn Somalia and drought-stricken Ethiopia lived. The small town was a place of desperate survivors, all with their own fierce struggles.

We headed to a campsite just outside the town owned by a Swiss man, Henry, who had married a local woman. Henry welcomed us, and we set up camp among the thorn trees. The primitive camp offered us a small shelter, potable water, and a long drop toilet.

Using a long drop, also known as a pit latrine, can often be an adventure in itself. The walls and even the hole in the ground attract all kinds of critters and bugs. Snakes curl up and hide in the thick grass walls, or if the walls are built with wood, the snakes hang out in the gaps and ledges of the unaligned wooden slats. Frogs hang out in the moisture, and rodents scurry across the floor. I was always concerned that something was going to jump up and bite my bum.

Tom and I lounged in our chairs, breathing easier after a grueling day of driving. I swatted away the hordes of irritating flies but was pleased that we had made it safely this far. Then I smelled fuel.

"It's nothing," Tom said. "They probably spilled some fuel when they filled the auxiliary tank." He sipped on his beer.

"The smell's strong. It's coming from the side opposite the fuel intake," I replied. "You need to check under the car."

Reluctantly, Tom crawled under the Cruiser. "Shit!" he yelled. "We've got a fuel leak from the spare tank, and I can't see where it's coming from," He emerged oily and dusty. "I'll take it to a garage first thing tomorrow and put the car over a pit, so I can get a better view. We can't drive until I figure out how serious the leak is." He dusted himself off. "As if this damn road isn't bloody difficult enough, and now this."

In the morning, Tom located a garage. The confident, clean-shaven mechanic wore grease-stained, dusty brown overalls and a cap pulled down over his ears. The garage looked like a wrecking yard: rusted car frames, chassis, axles, and other unrecognizable car parts lay scattered around the grease-soaked dirt. The work area consisted of corrugated iron sheets held up by wooden poles.

Tom reversed into a spot beside the remains of a green truck. All that was left in the battered green cab's steering wheel were the letters "OYO." The vehicle had probably once been a Toyota. Another man appeared wearing a floppy pink hat and grease-stained blue overalls. They had no pit, so a mechanic slunk down onto his belly and crawled under the Cruiser. While beneath the Cruiser, he cried out, "I find the leak and can fix it."

The hole had to be repaired before we could continue, so Tom gave them the go-ahead. They first had to drain forty gallons of fuel. A man with a hose, a large plastic red barrel, and a strong set of lungs sucked hard, and the fuel began to flow from the fuel tank into the barrel.

He spat out the fuel from his mouth and said, "Good, it comes."

Once empty, the men removed the fuel tank from the Cruiser and washed it out with soap and water. Then the repairs began. The cause of the leak, we soon discovered, was truly frightening: The mount holding the exhaust pipe to the chassis had broken loose due to the road corrugations. The exhaust pipe, hanging loose, had rubbed against the tank and worn away the metal, leaving a series of tiny holes. Fortunately, the exhaust pipe itself was still okay; otherwise, the high-temperature exhaust gases would have been blown directly into a flammable tank, which would have caused an explosion. We had been driving a bomb. Another reminder of how fragile life is and how the distance between life and death is literally just a spark.

Needing to breathe in the African smells, to touch the hot, dusty red soil with my bare feet, to taste the sweaty salt on my lips and hear the chatter of children, I walked out of the garage compound—more than ever, I was grateful to be alive. If I hadn't insisted Tom check under the car, we could have been blown off the planet, and nobody would ever have known what had happened to us.

After a long walk, I returned to the garage. The mechanics had braised the holes closed, welded on a steel patch to reinforce the weakened area, and reinstalled the repaired tank. They replaced the broken exhaust mount and siphoned back the fuel.

We returned to our campsite, immensely grateful that the tank had been repaired. Sipping on a can of Coke, I relaxed and settled under a large thorn tree to read and write. Tom made supper while the sun disappeared below the horizon. He lit candles because we'd found that candles attracted fewer mosquitoes than lanterns.

Suddenly my mouth exploded in searing pain, and I struggled to breathe. Gasping, I cried out, "Help me! I've been stung in my mouth." My can of Coke had attracted bees, and when I drank the cola, I got a mouthful of the angry insects.

"Take out the stings," I cried, thrusting my tongue out.

Tom managed to take two stings out of my tongue, but he couldn't reach the stings lodged in my throat. My tongue and throat started to swell. Struggling to breathe, I lay down in the dirt.

"Don't panic. Keep breathing." Tom sounded frantic, but I tried to follow his advice.

Closing my eyes, I sought to will the pain and swelling away. I sucked at the air. Pain seared through my mouth and throat. I gulped and closed my eyes, and the night closed in. *I'm going to die*, I thought.

"Jan, Jan, speak to me." Tom pulled me up to a sitting position. "Here's some water. Drink!"

Pushing his hand away, I focused on my breathing. My muscles tingled and began to relax. Eventually, the breathing grew easier. I opened my eyes. Tom stood over me and asked, "You okay?"

I nodded yes and lay quietly on the ground for several minutes, feeling the earth beneath me.

That night, as the wind stirred the dust, loud, noisy cicadas buzzed, and crickets clicked. I looked at the millions of stars, and I remembered the day—which now seemed an eternity ago—that I decided to walk away from my life. "You could die," friends had told me. And Tom had said the same thing. But then, deep down, I already felt dead, and the only way I could claim my life back was to take the risk I had taken and walk away from my monotonous and arid lifestyle. Though frightening, bee stings were, and are, less painful and less deadly to me than boredom and a sense of emptiness.

We set off on the final 155 miles to Moyale at the Ethiopian border early in the morning, a twelve-hour drive. The world passed by slowly, dust swirled about us, and it felt like the Cruiser was bouncing on a trampoline.

I opened my window, and the dust rushed in. Tom asked me to close it.

"I'm bored," I said. "And I'm tired of talking to you."

"What's wrong with talking to me?"

"Nothing. But what's left for us to talk about? We've discussed everything."

We had already discussed what we would do if we came back to earth as Jesus, Buddha, or Mohammed. We had come up with potential solutions for all the world's challenges. We had planned our funerals, chosen the music, and written our obituaries.

At a loss for further topics, I asked, "Where does a thought go when someone says, 'I've lost my thought'?" Tom said he wished I had a mute button on my forehead because he was tired of all my constant questions.

We hoped to cross into Ethiopia before the border closed, anxious to get the experience over with. According to stories, we'd heard that Moyale, on the Kenyan side, was a desperate, grubby town experiencing instability and frequent clashes over access to water and grazing land. As we drove toward the town, children threw rocks and stones at us, and teenagers flashed crude signs. We slowed down as they swarmed toward us on the road. A disheveled man holding a large object ran up, shouting at us.

"This is not good." Tom swiveled his head from side to side. His eyes searched for a way out as he drove toward the border.

The small threatening crowd parted enough to allow us to pass, but then more youngsters joined the group, screaming at us.

"There's got to be a police station somewhere here," Tom said. "Can you see it anywhere?"

My stomach twisted in knots. "I think it's over there." I pointed to a small building on the right. Tom turned and stopped in front of the police station. The crowd of restless young men watched as we parked and went inside. The policeman at the desk informed us that the border had closed and that we'd have to spend the night in Kenya. Tom asked where we might safely camp but received only a shrug at our apprehension in return. The policeman pointed to his left and said there was a fenced area where we should be safe. We returned to our Cruiser; the crowd of young men had gone. "There's a track leading off to the left," said Tom. "I'll go head down there."

Shortly after driving down the track, we saw a rickety, falling-down fence with several skinny cows behind it. We assumed this to be the fence the policeman had referred to. However, I had no idea how this fragile structure would offer us any safety. We managed to find the owner of the land, an older man who said we could camp on his property. As we set up our tent, I squeezed all thoughts of possible danger from my mind. I reassured myself that we'd be in Ethiopia in a few hours and that the worst part of our journey was behind us.

Chapter 14
A Handle for God

Ethiopia, 2006

After several days of tense driving through the volatile and risky area of northern Kenya, my whole body relaxed as soon as we crossed into Ethiopia. And yet a strange dislocation ensued since Ethiopian time is different; the twenty-four-hour day starts at sunrise, not midnight. Ethiopia also bases its year on the Julian calendar of thirteen months. We left Kenya in 2006 and arrived in Ethiopia in 1999. We seemed to have crossed more than an ordinary border. Perhaps I thought the country ahead would prove just as surprising.

Ethiopia is landlocked in the horn of Africa, with an estimated population of approximately ninety million. Over eighty languages and two hundred dialects are spoken there. The official language, Amharic, which we could neither speak nor read, has its own script. Because Ethiopia was never successfully colonized—although the Germans, Italians, and British certainly tried—the local languages were never colonized. They remained Semitic languages with a Middle Eastern origin. In brief, the resilient Ethiopians never gave up their fight against colonialism and never gave up their languages.

At the border, a polite and efficient official approached us and told me to drive into a fenced courtyard so he could inspect our vehicle. Young children, mostly boys but some girls, stood outside the courtyard behind the wire-mesh fence, pointing at us and calling out, "*Farangi*"—foreigner—"you, you, you!" I waved back to them, and they screeched with delight even more when I asked them if I could take their photos.

As we drove toward Addis Ababa, the capital, it seemed I'd not only entered a new country but had also been transported back several centuries. A woman wearing a long flowing kaftan and scarves draped over her head sat sideways on a donkey while a man who walked alongside wore a loose-fitting cotton shirt, long pants, and leather sandals. I thought of the scenes in the New Testament of Joseph walking beside Mary, riding along on a donkey.

As the landscape unspooled past us, Tom and I discussed the last two days of our journey. We had struggled to come to an agreement on whether to drive the northern Kenya road without a convoy. And I still wondered whether going without a convoy had been the right decision.

"I think we were just fortunate that nothing serious happened," I said.

"We're damn lucky that the fuel tank didn't explode, and that we could get it repaired."

"I was lucky I didn't die from the bee stings."

Each day I faced new experiences. Emotions entirely new to me would bubble to the surface. How was I supposed to feel? Words eluded me, and I distracted myself by watching the road ahead, which cut a path through golden yellow fields that rolled over the hills and disappeared into the blue horizon.

Large beehive-shaped piles of yellow hay dotted the landscape. In the distance, farmers and their families harvested tef—a grain similar to millet and the main cereal of Ethiopians. Wiry young boys, some barefoot, walked alongside the road carrying bundles of hay often larger than themselves.

Dust clung to the slender but muscular, sweaty bodies of youngsters in the fields, who, with a quick movement, slashed the crop with their sickles. Others raked the cuttings into enormous piles. Cattle, led by men, threshed the harvest by trampling over it, walking around and around in circles. Women repeatedly tossed the freshly cut crop with pitchforks back beneath the hooves of cows and bullocks, a process separating the tef from the stems, which are used as hay to feed the cattle.

We slowed down as we approached a small village, eventually stopping at a little tin shack. As we entered the busy stall, the smell of freshly roasted coffee and a blaring TV in the corner greeted us. Eager to try the well-known Ethiopian coffee, we ordered a macchiato. We sat down, and when I glanced up at the TV, the grainy gray picture of a young girl belting out a song on *Ethiopian Idol* brought me back to reality. Culture creep had reached the heart of Africa.

Several days later, we arrived in Addis Ababa, a sprawling city of over three million people with a kaleidoscopic mixture of modern buildings, luxury homes, and run-down shacks. On the outskirts of Addis, we switched drivers, as I always drove in the cities. Now, ready to tackle the chaotic confusion of driving into the capital, I revved the engine and, most importantly, tested the brakes. Tom scrolled through the GPS coordinates. "Stay on this road. Keep heading north."

I rolled down my window and adjusted my side mirror. "And then?"

"At Meskel Square, turn left. The Baro Hotel is a few blocks from there."

Dust and diesel fumes hopped into the Cruiser for a ride. I rolled up my window. "Tom, please adjust your side mirror so I can see the traffic."

He rolled down his window and reached for the mirror. "How's that?" he asked. I nodded, and he rolled his window back up. "You ready for this?"

I turned on the air conditioner. "Yes," I said.

We faced a new challenge in Ethiopia; traffic drove on the right side of the road. Our Cruiser was right-hand drive, so the passenger—in

this case, Tom—now sat where the steering wheel should be and had
to decide when it was safe for me to overtake. He also had to watch
oncoming traffic and warn me if I needed to swerve to avoid a collision. Fortunately, by this point, we had already gained several days
of driving experience in Ethiopia. Nevertheless, our ability to work
well together while navigating unfamiliar roads across a city remained
essential.

"I'm ready," Tom said. "Let's go."

Our teamwork paid off, and after driving several miles into the
city, I relaxed, despite the chaos. Hundreds of blue-and-white Kombi
and Toyota Corolla taxis weaved in and out between trucks, buses,
cars, and donkey carts. Men and women dodged and scampered
between the fast-moving traffic.

"Donkeys are running on the side of the road," I said.

"Keep going. We're doing well," Tom said. "In about half a mile,
we'll be at Meskel Square. Keep to the right."

But it wouldn't have mattered which side of the road I chose;
the Meskel intersection was a chaotic maze of vehicles going in all
directions.

"Good luck," Tom said as our Cruiser crawled into the intersection.

An angry green truck farted pungent black fumes at our fog lights.
I looked around for traffic lights, police officers, or even a yield or stop
sign—nothing. Young boys leaned out the windows of yellow buses
and Kombi taxis, yelling and laughing. I slammed the brakes on, and
our seatbelts grabbed us. "Holy moly," I muttered. Vehicles entered
the intersection, all coming from different directions. Three buses in
convoy, bumper to bumper, wormed their way through traffic like a
yellow snake. A man sitting on the top of a moving black truck waved
to several people who dared to risk their lives running across the road,
weaving and dodging between the oncoming traffic. Suddenly I found
my courage, and our Cruiser roared into the center of the fray.

I steered through the shifting maze of vehicles and people,

constantly tensed for impact, my eyes straining to pick out the greatest danger in all the motion. Finally, after what seemed like hours
but was only minutes, we made it through Ethiopia's notorious
accident-hotspot intersection without a nudge, a bump, or a scrape.
Afterward, finding our accommodation was mere child's play.

The manager of the budget hotel allowed us to camp in the parking lot and pay to use a shower or toilet. We set up our rooftop tent
and then went for a pizza supper, one of the many dishes left behind
by the Italians when they tried to colonize the country.

We returned in the darkness, climbed up to our tent, and lay
awake listening to the constant comings and goings in the parking lot.
Cars arrived and left, doors opened and banged shut, and there were
loud discussions and laughter.

In the morning, Tom said, "I suggest we book a room. The parking lot is too damn noisy."

He left to find the manager and returned several minutes later,
chuckling to himself.

"The manager wants to know how long you wanted the room for."
Tom was laughing so hard it took him several seconds before he spluttered out the question. "Thirty minutes? One hour?"

I sniggered. "Tom, you know you only need ten minutes; I need
at least thirty."

Once we managed to compose ourselves, we agreed we would get
used to the noise and would sleep in our tent. The parking lot was
obviously also a meeting place for many locals on other businesses.
Hawkers wandered through, selling their wares (fresh bread, tomatoes, large brown eggs) to the steady stream of visitors and travelers.

While standing in the shade of a bushy green tree in the parking
lot one afternoon, I watched a young woman with combs, strings of
beads, and a pair of scissors neatly laid out on a piece of cardboard at
her feet; she was braiding another woman's hair. Since I hadn't had a
haircut since leaving Canada, I approached her and asked if she'd cut

my hair. She smiled, said yes, and then offered to braid my hair with pretty, colorful beads.

"No, my hair is too skinny," I said.

She laughed as she ran her fingers through my fine, sun-bleached straight hair.

"Not too short," I said, sitting on the wooden crate with the familiar Coca-Cola red swirls (but obviously written in Amharic). Several other women also wanted to feel my head. They giggled and chatted among themselves as their fingers moved gently through my limp hair. Wonderfully relaxed, I stretched out my tanned legs, crossed my ankles, closed my eyes, and reminded the young woman, "Not too short." As my hair tumbled down my nose and cheeks, I pursed my lower lip out and blew hard upward. Suddenly, a car arrived, and we had to move. The hairdresser carried the crate and the tools of her trade across the parking lot. A moment later, I sat back down so she could finish the job. After a while, she stepped back.

"Finished," she said, then whipped out a red cloth and dusted me off.

I moved my hands up to the top of my head to find short hair much shorter than I had expected. Consoling myself that it would be months before I would need another haircut, I paid the woman and returned to our Cruiser.

"What the hell have you done to your head?" Tom asked.

I shrugged. "I should have had my hair braided with pretty string beads. Oh well, next time." I could already tell that Addis was a city of fresh opportunities.

The sprawling capital is best known for its vibrant culture, people, and quality of food rather than its sights. I was eager to visit the National Museum at the university to see Lucy. This fossil skeleton had rewritten the story of humanity. Discovered in 1974 in Hadar, Ethiopia, Lucy, according to recent estimates, is more than three million years old—at that time, the oldest early human ever found.

Apparently, the anthropologists named the fossil after the Beatles' song "Lucy in the Sky with Diamonds," which was playing at their campsite the evening after the discovery. I wondered if the anthropologists were as surprised as I was at how tiny Lucy was as an adult. She would have been just over three feet and weighed about sixty-four pounds. The actual bones, however, are preserved in the museum's archives, and what we saw was only a cast of her skeletal fragments.

Even so, the experience was profoundly moving. I thought long and hard about how science has changed how we experience and see the world. I was intrigued by the thought that we are all descendants of those ancient ancestors and are all linked to the birthplace of humankind, Africa.

Tom and I stepped out of the museum into the sunshine and walked along a pathway lined by tall shady green trees, past casually dressed students making their way to and from lectures. Lovers held hands, giggled, and whispered to one another. Others lounged on the grass in the shade of the trees, chatting, arguing, and laughing loudly. I so regretted not being able to understand the language. If I'd been able to talk to the students, I would have had a much richer experience of their country. Speaking and understanding more global languages would obviously have a dramatic effect on the way any of us experience the world. Frustrated by my inability to communicate with the students, I promised myself that, in my next life, I would be a polyglot.

We strolled across the campus and returned to our Cruiser. Tom suggested that we find a place to have lunch. Rumor had it that the Addis Ababa Sheraton served great hamburgers, so we decided to treat ourselves. While driving to the hotel, I stopped at a traffic light. Tom leaned out of the window and gave money to someone I couldn't see. When I asked what he was doing, he answered, "A kid is begging. He's so badly crippled he can't stand up properly."

Earlier on the trip, we had agreed to give money only to disabled persons or people who'd helped us, so I took Tom's generosity in stride. However, as I drove away, I glanced in the side mirror and laughed at what I saw.

"Hey, look at the kid you just gave money to," I said.

The boy had stood up and removed a cardboard hump from under his shirt.

Tom turned and looked in his side mirror at the boy and chuckled. "Well, you've got to admire his ingenuity."

I shook my head. "When it comes to survival skills, these kids would run circles around our kids back home."

Clean white Land Cruisers—the property of various NGOs and UN agencies—filled the parking lot of the Sheraton. We parked our dirty, scratched, and dented Land Cruiser. I slunk into the lobby, hoping nobody would notice how scruffy I looked, especially with my new haircut.

I ordered my lunch. The hamburger arrived on a gold-rimmed white plate with silver cutlery. As I bit into the crisp fresh lettuce, sweet red tomatoes, and juicy patty, my taste buds danced with delight, even though I knew the $12 hamburger cost more than many locals earned in a day. But my curiosity got the better of me as I wondered how much a room cost for a night. After lunch, we returned to the foyer, and I approached the reception desk.

"How much for a room?"

The young receptionist, wearing a blue blazer, raised her perfectly plucked eyebrows. Her eyes grew wide, and she looked me up and down before leaning forward over the polished desk and softly whispering, "It's very expensive."

I glanced down at my grubby self, ran my fingers through my remaining chopped hair, and then repeated in my poshest accent, "How much?" I learned later that the price of a few nights' stay equaled a policeman's annual salary.

Outside the hotel, a wall painted with pretty scenes surrounded the large swimming pool area reserved for privileged guests. Some sunbathed while others swam in the clean pool. Nobody had to see what was on the other side of the painted wall. We returned to our Cruiser in the parking lot and wondered again about the role of foreign aid and NGOs.

We had met some dedicated workers and volunteers and seen their tremendous work. But we had also seen the unintended consequences: the resultant lack of accountability by politicians and their dependency on aid. Addis Ababa is the headquarters of the Africa Union and has one of the highest numbers of NGOs in the world. The boy with the hump who saw our white Land Cruiser knew what he had to do to get money from us. He had obviously assumed that we were NGO workers and took a chance that he would receive a generous handout. We were often mistaken for NGO workers because white Land Cruisers are the most common vehicles driven by foreign NGOs, charities, and aid agencies.

After several days of rest, exploring the city, and restocking our supplies, we packed up and left Addis Ababa. The road north wound through the forests and over the Entoto Mountains. Women permanently bent from years of carrying heavy loads of eucalyptus wood on their backs shuffled slowly down the road to the city below. Strong young men jogged their way up the steep incline. Heavily laden donkeys trotted ahead of men glistening with sweat who waved sticks in the air to direct the donkeys between the traffic and people. Late that afternoon, we arrived in the small city of Bahir Dar, situated on the shores of Lake Tana, Ethiopia's largest lake and the source of the Blue Nile.

We hiked along a rocky path to the Blue Nile Falls, downstream from the lake. The water plunges over the 148-foot fall and flows nearly one thousand miles through canyons, gorges, and deserts, carrying with it fertile silt that is the lifeline for millions living along the Nile. Later the Blue Nile meets up with the White Nile just south of Khartoum in Sudan.

At the waterfalls, a blue butterfly with a yellow stripe on its wings caught my eye. I watched it play in the breeze and mist, flitting between the stems of the grass. Then I saw a young girl about fourteen years old wearing a faded red dress, being led by a girl of about seven years old. The girl in the red dress clutched the arm of the littler girl, who was leading her down a pathway. Immediately, I suspected the girl in the red dress, who had a silver cross hanging from a piece of black string tied around her neck, suffered from river blindness, her eyes destroyed by worms transmitted through the repeated bites of infectious blackflies. This disease, onchocerciasis, is the second leading infectious cause of blindness worldwide, and 99 percent of infected people live in Africa. People most likely to suffer from this disease live in remote rural agricultural villages close to fast-flowing streams.

The butterfly flew in front of the blind girl, but only the girl leading her looked up to see the beautiful blue butterfly with a yellow stripe on its wings.

Then the younger child glanced at me. The expression in her dark brown eyes suggested that she was unsure about me. Her smooth dark skin was almost gray with dirt. A band of soft black curls framed her small pretty face, but the rest of her hair had been shaved off except on the top of her head, where a small tuft of soft black curls remained. I had previously been told that this particular haircut was done so that God would have a handle should he decide to take the child home.

With the waterfall's roar behind me and the cool mist on my back, I watched the two children walk away. I thought about the mothers in the area. Did they weep when they cut their children's hair and left handles for God? I thought about my mother, knowing that if I had died as a child, she would have wept, and maybe my father would have too. But mostly, I thought about my sons and how I used to cut their hair. Doing so, I never had to think about my children perhaps dying one day. I never had to consider leaving a handle for God.

Hiking back in silence, I recalled my years working as a pediatric nurse at the Alberta Children's Hospital, where, on several occasions, I had witnessed the unbearable pain of a parent when their child dies. Nothing can ever prepare a parent for the death of their young child, especially when it is sudden and unexpected—not even a handle for God; of that, I am sure.

Later that day, Tom and I walked down to the lake to purchase freshly caught tilapia for our supper. Men in traditional papyrus-reed canoe-shaped boats paddled across the lake, the boats so low that it looked as if the men and their loads of goods were floating on the surface. On land, the men heaved their reed boats out of the water and leaned them against trees and poles to dry. Because they aren't water-proof, the boats last only a few months and must be tended carefully. On the lake, flocks of pelicans swam gracefully past. They dipped their large long yellow beaks into the water to scoop up struggling fish and then tossed back their heads to swallow their catches. Fishermen on the lake edge repaired their reed boats. They sorted their catches of tilapia and catfish while chatting loudly with one another. An old gray-haired man sat idly by, watching as noisy children laughed and played.

A gentle breeze cooled the air in the town of Gondar, known as the Camelot of Africa due to its seventeenth-century palaces, crenelated castles, and churches behind the tall basalt stone walls of the Royal Enclosure. Young men and boys, dressed in long pants and shirts and often with green shawls wrapped around them, herded oxen down the rocky dirt road past the crumbling stone walls. Women in long kaftans, with thin white cloths draped over their faces like bridal veils, hung their washing on tree branches and over rickety wood fences. The Belegez Pension, which lies within walking distance of the Royal Enclosure, allowed us to camp in their small parking lot.

Wandering through the Royal Enclosure, we enjoyed the calm stillness. We admired the eighty Ethiopian cherubs, each with a different expression, painted on the ceiling of the Debre Berhan Selassie

Church. But our most desired destination lay in the mountainous region of northern Ethiopia, where the remote and isolated town of Lalibela, a UNESCO World Heritage Site, is located. We decided to fly there rather than drive. Lalibela, a village of Ethiopian Orthodox Christianity, is a place of pilgrimage and sanctity. Eleven churches carved out of volcanic rock in the thirteenth century lie deep within giant open pits. The churches had been built this way so as not to be visible from afar; the earth, in other words, hid the places of worship from the view of enemies.

During the ninety-minute flight to Lalibela, I looked down at the land below. I wondered if I was seeing the same fields I first saw in the western media during the 1984 Ethiopian famine. Who could forget those haunting photographs of starving infants, children, and adults that had shocked the world? But remembering images is an easy salve on the conscience and, without action, is of little use to those who suffer. What, I wondered, had the Ethiopian leaders done with the millions of dollars that had flowed into their country after the world was made aware of the unfolding tragedy?

After a bumpy flight and landing, I was pleased to be back on solid ground. Mesfin, our guide, wearing a white shirt with a blue sweater casually slung over his shoulders, greeted us in perfect English and radiated so much warmth that I took an instant liking to him. He was in his late twenties, of medium height with a slim build, and was cleanly shaven except for a thin mustache. Tom and I followed him up a hill to our hotel, which had more fleas than guests, and Mesfin agreed to meet up with us later after we had settled in.

The tourist office was closed, and few tourists were around. In fact, we had the town of fewer than eight thousand inhabitants almost to ourselves. With Mesfin guiding us, we spent several relaxed days in the area, exploring the thirteen monolithic churches chiseled out of the soft red volcanic rock. We watched priests wearing flowing white gowns and turbans moved slowly through a chapel, singing to the rhythmic beat of drums. Their melodic chants echoed off the rock ceiling and painted frescoes on the rock walls. A sweet aroma from the flickering beeswax candles in the dark drifted around me. The chanting grew louder and faster as the priests walked toward the large wooden doors.

In the evening, we sat beneath a moonless sky swarming with stars and, with several men, enjoyed a traditional meal of injera and stew. They asked us why we'd flown and not driven to Lalibela. Tom said we'd heard that some children throw stones at cars from the roadside.

The discussion slumped into silence until an older man spoke wearily. "You taught our children to beg. Before you came, our children never begged. They were not a problem." He paused, his voice even heavier than before. "Now, it is difficult for us."

I asked him what his government had done with the international money raised after the famine. He shook his head and said he didn't know. I thought of the boy with his cardboard hump and the children who called out, "*Farangi, farangi*, you, you, you," to get our attention.

And I knew that Tom and I represented the "you"—the foreigner.

Having grown up and lived in South Africa, I understood the sadness in the older man's voice, the despair brought on by the knowledge that the outside world continually rushes in with its western solutions for Africa's challenges. The complexities of the different cultures, traditions, beliefs, values, and even legal systems are either ignored or misunderstood. I felt a knot of sadness that despite my roots, I would always be viewed as an outsider on this continent, a "you"—a *farangi*.

After our return to Gondar, we decided it was time to leave Ethiopia and head for the Sudan border 124 miles away. We were excited. Sudan was the last country we would travel through before reaching Egypt, and our final destination of Cairo, ending our journey from Cape Town to Cairo. We chatted as we packed the Cruiser, wondering what Sudan would be like.

It was February 2006, and violent protests against the Danish cartoons that offensively depicted the Prophet Mohammed had spread across the Muslim world. Having heard reports of escalating violence, we removed the red-and-white Canadian flag on our Cruiser in case it was mistaken for a Danish red-and-white flag. Nevertheless, we waved goodbye to our fellow travelers and headed eagerly to Al Qadarif in Sudan. We planned to be at Gallabat, on the Ethiopia-Sudan border, by lunchtime.

I drove slowly, my view often obscured by the dust kicked up by overloaded buses, donkey carts, and other vehicles. Goats, cows, donkeys, and chickens constantly wandered across the dirt road, as did people—women carrying bundles of firewood or jugs of water, children playing, and men socializing. I relaxed behind the wheel, with excited anticipation of approaching the border of a new country.

"We're making good time—only eighteen miles to the border," Tom said as he began to sort our documents. "Passports, insurance, vaccination certificates, Cruiser documents. We're ready."

"We've just passed the last village," I replied. "Nearly time to say goodbye to Ethiopia. We've had a great time here."

Tom pointed ahead to some children playing on the road. "Watch those kids."

"Yeah, I see them." I slowed to about seven miles per hour and honked at the group of approximately twenty children and a few adults. They all dispersed to the side of the dirt road.

Suddenly a small child turned back and ran in front of our Cruiser. I slammed my foot hard on the brakes and spun the wheel sharply in a desperate attempt to avoid the child, now directly in our path. My world jolted to a stop. The child grabbed the bull bar. His eyes, wide with terror, locked on mine. He was so tiny that I could see only his head above the bar. Then he disappeared beneath the Cruiser as if jerked down by invisible hands.

Chapter 15
Tragedy and Heartbreak

Ethiopia, February 2006

I tasted dust in my mouth as I hung over the wheel, gazing wildly through the windshield, waiting for the child to stand up. A crescendo of screams and shouts of rage filled my ears—an overloaded passenger bus had stopped behind us. Despite my panic and horror, I heard the voices in my head of fellow travelers who had told us, "Never stop if you have an accident. It is much too dangerous. Go straight to the nearest police station."

Tom grabbed the door handle. "I'll go see."

Before I could say anything, he opened the Cruiser door and climbed out. The crowd swarmed him, and I watched, terrified, as he vanished into the mob. In numbed disbelief at what had just happened, I somehow managed to open my door and follow. The crowd parted and allowed me to make my way to the front of the Cruiser. The small body lay still in the dirt and blood. His ripped-off scalp exposed his bloodied white skull. As he struggled to breathe, he blew tiny bubbles of blood and mucus out of his nose. I ran to the back of the Cruiser and tried desperately to pull out the medical kit tucked beneath our luggage.

"Tom! I need help!" I screamed, but my yells disappeared into the noise of the crowd.

Suddenly the medical kit came free, and I ran back to the child. Every cell in my brain told me to put on gloves, but my fear of the child dying consumed me, and I didn't waste time bothering with the

165

protective protocol. I knelt beside the boy and wiped the blood from his mouth and nose. I shut out the thunderous roars of the crowd, the dust, the heat, and even the smell of death as my nurse's instincts took over. Gently moving the child's head, I put my right hand into the warm pool of blood collected between his skull and his scalp and began removing stones, pebbles, and other debris. My fingers worked quickly to remove the dirt-laden blood before I carefully placed the scalp back over the child's skull. Reaching into the medical kit, I took out the bandages and wrapped the child's head tightly to stop the bleeding. I glanced up. Tom was standing at my side. His eyes wide with fear and horror, he grasped the top of his head, his face drained of all color.

"Bring me a blanket and pick him up, but don't move his neck and back," I said as I looked up at Tom. "I'll drive, you hold the child, and we'll go back to the village."

Tom wrapped the child in a blanket and climbed into the passenger seat. I started the Cruiser. The crowd refused to move. Their yells in Amharic needed no translation. They didn't want us to leave. They hit the Cruiser with sticks and pummeled it with their fists. Their cries and yells overwhelmed my senses. I gripped the wheel harder to stop my hands and body from shaking. Suddenly a man pushed his way through the crowd to the front. Yelling, he smashed his fist against Tom's window and grabbed the door handle.

"Look," I said. "That man is trying to get into the Cruiser. He's crying. Maybe it's the child's father. Let him in."

The sobbing man climbed in beside Tom. Small and thin, the man looked so fragile it seemed that he would break. He swayed back and forth as his fists beat his head, and he howled with pain.

The crowd parted. I turned the Cruiser around and headed back to Metema, the last village. All I could do now was concentrate on the road ahead and the need to get the injured child medical help. The father continued to cry loudly. None of us spoke. Words would have been useless anyway.

I had heard that when a vehicle hits a pedestrian in Ethiopia, the driver is considered guilty and is usually charged as such. I would go to jail until a settlement was reached. But even as those thoughts flashed through my mind, all I could do was concentrate on the road ahead and the need to get the child medical help. I stayed focused and listened to the father weep.

Tom gently closed the child's eyes.

I turned and looked at the boy. "Stay with me, stay with me," I begged. "Please stay. Please stay with me."

"The child's dying," Tom whispered. He rocked the child tenderly against his chest.

"Oh, God, no. He can't. Please don't let him die." I thought of our remote location and wondered if there even was a clinic at Metema.

As I turned off the road into the village, I heard Tom say, "He's gone! I heard his last breath. A deep sigh."

"Oh, God. Please, no," I cried.

I stopped the Cruiser and leaned out the window and asked the people walking around, "Where is the clinic?" but nobody answered. The father couldn't help—he was unable to find words between his sobs and cries of pain.

I saw a building with a corrugated tin roof that looked like a clinic. A row of rooms opened onto a veranda on which groups of people mingled. Many were coughing; some struggled to walk. Others carried crying babies. I drove up to the building, jumped out of the Cruiser, and ran in. Tom followed, carrying the lifeless child. A slim-built young male nurse appeared wearing a casual open-neck shirt and long pants.

Pointing with his stethoscope to a battered, bare metal stretcher, his voice barely audible, he said in broken English, "Put child there."

I explained to the nurse what had happened. Calm and unhurried, he listened quietly and asked no questions. Tom placed the limp child on the stretcher, and the nurse pressed his stethoscope on the child's bony chest.

I waited. All my focus was on the nurse, who had closed his eyes as if in deep concentration. I watched him reposition the stethoscope on the child's chest, searching for life. I sucked in the stale air, and time seemed to stop.

Then the nurse pulled the blanket over the child's face, stepped back, and said, "He's dead."

"No," I cried and pulled the blanket back down. Desperately searching for a pulse, I put my ear on the child's chest and listened, but the only sounds I heard were the wailing sobs of the father and the shouts and murmurs of a gathering crowd. I replaced the blanket over the child's body.

A big-boned man wearing a white lab coat entered the room. "I am here to determine the cause of death." His voice was harsh and angry, and he held the lapels of his coat as he glared at me. "And then, you will be held fully accountable."

He pulled the blanket down. Without touching the child, he glanced at the bandaged head and said, "He died of intracranial bleeding." The doctor pulled the blanket up over the child's face again and turned to leave. Finally overwhelmed as the reality of the situation hit me, I broke down and began to weep quietly.

"Why are you crying?" the doctor demanded. "Children die all the time. If he hadn't died today, he would have died later of malnutrition or disease. I see it every day. So stop crying."

I walked to the father, who stood in the doorway, and held out my hand. "I am so sorry."

He hung his head low, and his painful wails pierced through me. I placed my palms together and covered my mouth with my fingers in an agonizing torment of guilt.

Feeling a steady hand on my shoulder, I turned around. Through the blur of my tears, I saw the nurse. His dark eyes voiced concerns.

"What will happen now?" I asked.

He wiped away little beads of sweat on his brow with the back of his hand. "You will have to pay compensation to the child's family. But you might not have to be in jail for long." He lowered his voice and spoke slowly and gently. "Maybe not even a year."

I looked down and saw I had blood on my shoes. I must have stepped in the child's blood. *Oh, God*, I thought, *who was he?* I looked at the nurse and asked, "What's the child's name?"

The nurse turned to the father and spoke in Amharic. "Getaw," the nurse said, turning back. "His name was Getaw."

"Getaw," I whispered. "I'm so sorry. I'm so, so sorry."

Tom started to ask the nurse, "How . . . ," but hesitated. Letting out a heavy breath, he finally completed his question. "How much compensation would be reasonable?" Tom's eyes filled with anxiety and his face flushed.

Nauseated and even more numb than before, I glanced at my shaking, bloodied hands and slowly crossed the room to the sink. I could hardly grasp the enormity of the conversation. How could any amount of money be put on the life of a child?

"Three thousand dollars would be good," the nurse replied.

I heard Tom breathing deeply, but he said nothing.

I wanted to wash the blood off my hands in the small, dirty sink, but when I turned on the taps, no water came out.

I turned to the nurse and said, "I need to go to the toilet."

He pointed to four open-air wooden enclosures at the end of the veranda.

I walked in the shade of the roof toward the enclosure. Mothers pulled their children out of my way. The men stopped speaking to one another when I passed them. I felt their wary eyes watching me. The stench of sweat permeated the hot air.

I entered the first enclosure, but shit covered the squat toilet, and there was nowhere to put my feet. I didn't want to go outside and face the people again, so I bent down and passed through a small hole in the wall into the enclosure behind it. Flies buzzed around a putrid blend of shit, piss, vomit, and blood. I felt as if I had been locked out of my consciousness. Nothing seemed to make sense. In all my life, I'd never felt such a stultifying weight of anguish.

I returned to the room where Tom was, but the nurse stood sideways in the doorway, speaking to the milling crowd outside. The nurse had short dark hair and an oval face. His eyes were very dark brown, and he had a thin mustache. He spoke with authority to the restless crowd.

"Anteneh," said Tom, pointing to the nurse, "said he'll stay with us until the police arrive."

"Thank you, Anteneh," I said.

Anteneh nodded his head. "You be safe here."

I looked at the bed. The child's body was gone.

Two young policemen arrived. They told me they would take me away to a safe place because the people were enraged that I had killed the boy. They led me off and locked me alone in a room. Angry shouts and cries from the restless crowd outside washed in waves against the walls.

Hunched over in a battered wooden chair, my head in my hands, I felt utterly listless, my body drained of energy and my mouth parched. I looked up feebly as the doctor entered the room. He towered over me and stabbed the air with his fingers, while the menacing ghost of his shadow danced on the grubby gray wall behind him.

"You're lucky they didn't put a bullet in your head. Now stop crying." Flies circled the single light bulb that hung from the ceiling. "Don't move. Just stay here. They don't know where you are. But if they find you, they might kill you." He turned and strode from the room, slamming the door behind him. The key clicked in the lock. Again, I was alone. I had no idea where Tom had been taken. Would I ever see him again? *Oh, God*, I thought, *what have I gotten us into?*

In the hot and dusty air, my body was sticky with sweat and tears. Struggling to cope with the accident and its aftermath, I prepared myself for the worst. Questions forced my mind into places I didn't want it to go.

"I'll do what's right, no matter what," I whispered to the emptiness. But when I looked again at the blood on my hands, my stomach heaved with waves of nausea and fear.

I looked at my watch—almost two in the afternoon. With a sickening sensation, I thought about how our day had started so ordinarily and how in an instant, our lives had been irrevocably changed. I closed my eyes and buried my head in the palms of my still-bloodied hands. The bitter, harsh smell of blood and dirt was overwhelming.

Several hours later, I heard voices and then a click, and the door opened. I looked up and saw Tom and the two policemen. Tom entered the room and walked over to me.

"Oh, God, Tom, what's happening?" I stood up but felt rooted to the ground.

He took my two arms. "It's going to be okay, but you've got to come with me."

"Where're we going?" My eyes glanced at the open door and the policemen who were blocking our way out. I heard a dog yapping in the distance.

"To the police station." He looked at the two policemen and then back at me. "They want to question you." I could hardly breathe, and I began to shiver.

In a stern voice, the younger policeman said aggressively, "Come. We go." He motioned us to follow them.

Tom put his arm around my shoulder, and we walked out of the room. Men watching us murmured among themselves and spoke to the police. Despite not being able to understand Amharic, their voices sounded angry, and my fear increased.

While walking to the Cruiser, Tom said he would drive to the police station. He also told me that he'd hired a local with a pickup truck to take the child's body and his father back to their village.

We all left in a convoy for the police station: the police, the truck with the child's body, and us in our Cruiser.

As we drove, Tom told me, "The police are going to arrest you." He reached out and patted my arm. "But I called the Canadian international-emergency number on our satellite phone. They put me through to the embassy in Addis Ababa, so they know what's happened."

"What did you tell them? What did they say?"

"I explained that we're Canadians traveling through Ethiopia and that we've had an accident in which a child has died. I told them I was with the police. They said they can't intervene in the legal process but that they would be following our case."

At the police compound, we parked our Cruiser under a large, leafy tree at the entrance. Once the father was certain we were in police custody, the truck with him and the child's body left for their village. I thought of Getaw's mother. Did she know her child was dead? Did she have other children? What if he was her only son or perhaps even her only child? I imagined her collapsing onto the ground in a convulsion of grief, her high-pitched wails echoing across the village. Women would rush to her side, and the children would begin to cry. I watched the truck with her child's body drive off, followed by a cloud of dust. A wave of nauseous pain and fear crashed over me. Tom took my hand, and we walked into the station.

The police station consisted of several offices around a dusty brown-earth courtyard. At the entrance, a group of about fifty men, women, and children stood in the shade of the tall eucalyptus tree. They quietly watched events unfold. Men talked among themselves, and young women with infants strapped to their backs seemed equally absorbed in the unfolding drama even as children played around, oblivious to the situation. Some men milled around our Land Cruiser, pointing to it and touching it.

We were given white plastic chairs to sit on in the courtyard while the five policemen talked among themselves. In the center of the courtyard stood a square wooden structure. Even from twenty feet away, I could hear people talking inside it. No one opened the door; the police simply shouted at the hidden people. I assumed that the structure was some sort of holding cell. Was that where I was going to be placed? Breathing deeply, I listened to my breath. The prospect of what lay ahead was overwhelming.

"Come." A policeman who spoke some English appeared and told us to follow him into the office. He was shorter than Tom and not as well built. He had short black hair, and his look was firm. His face was oval with deep-set eyes, and he had a small mole above his right eyebrow.

Smartly dressed in his khaki-colored police uniform, he positioned himself behind a desk and motioned us to sit in the two plastic chairs opposite. He reached into a drawer and pulled out a giant ledger. On the desk, untidy piles of paper were stacked alongside a black rotary-dial phone. A lightbulb hung by a wire from the ceiling, and the late-afternoon sun shone through a hole in the wall, the only window in the place. The policeman picked up a pen, and the questioning began. His dark eyes fixed on me.

"What your name? Where you from, and where you go?" A silver key chain attached to his belt clinked as he fiddled with it with his left hand.

Tom told him he knew the exact location of the accident because he had it marked on our GPS. But the policeman showed no interest in investigating the accident or in interviewing any witnesses. My fate was sealed. I had killed a child, and events would unfold under Ethiopian law. Was it true what I'd heard, that I could face a mandatory sentence of seventeen years in prison? I began to prepare myself for the inevitable, wondering whether I would be put in solitary confinement or with the general prison population. All at once, I felt a calm, fatalistic acceptance of my future. Indeed, I even hoped to be put in with the general prison population. At least then I could learn to speak Amharic.

The loud ring of the black rotary phone on the desk interrupted my thoughts. The policeman picked up the receiver and leaned back in his chair. He listened, nodded, then looked up at me and spoke to the caller in Amharic. We waited.

After several tense minutes, during which I wondered how Tom and I would cope if the police separated us, he put the phone down and leaned forward. "We take you to Gondar tomorrow. The district chief of police says the Canada government spoke to him. I take your passports and car. We keep you here tonight, and tomorrow you go to Gondar with the police. The chief will see you in Gondar."

We got up to leave.

"I take you to a safe place. Take from your car only what you need for the night. Then you cannot go back to your car; they may come back to kill you."

He walked us to a building in a complex hidden behind a high mud wall. A man opened the heavy metal gates, and we entered. We were taken to a small room at the end of the building and were reminded yet again that we couldn't leave, that we were in danger of a revenge attack.

The room had a heavy, scarred metal door and sliding bolt lock. A single bed with a gray threadbare blanket over the bare mattress was pushed up against the wall under a window. There was no other furniture, just a lonely gecko on the wall watching our every move; a slight breeze filtered through the window, which had metal bars but no glass. *Like a prison*, I thought as I stood on the cool cement floor. The room opened into a courtyard with a tree and plants. Women working there ignored us. I was not sure who they were. I made my way to the toilet and the sink, and, finally, I washed the blood from my hands.

Exhausted and overwhelmed, I lay down on the bed. Tom sat on the step of the doorway, his back to me. It was dusk. Gray wispy smoke rose in the distance, and the smells of suppers cooking over charcoal fires filled the evening air. I kept replaying the day's tragedy in my head and felt a strange terror at the thought of what the next day might hold in store for us. Would we be separated? Perhaps for years? Would Tom return to Canada, or would he stay in Ethiopia? What about my sons? What would they do?

Later, the policeman who had interviewed us arrived to ask how we were doing. Tom thanked him and offered to buy him a beer at the snack stall in the complex. The policeman smiled and said he would go home for supper and return later.

It was dark when two men in plain clothes arrived. One was the policeman, but I had no idea who the other man was. Once they were seated comfortably holding their beers, they told Tom he would have to pay the family compensation. Tom said that he'd been advised to pay the family $3,000. A child's high-pitched cry in the distance pierced the night air, and suddenly my mouth was full of bile. "I've got to go," I said. Tom looked at me with pain etched across his face, but he just nodded his head.

I returned to our room and lay on the bed. From this position, I could only listen to the words floating indistinctly in the dusty air.

The whole conversation, in any case, was difficult to follow due to translation challenges.

"Three thousand is too much," said the policeman.

"Well, you tell me how much," Tom replied.

"You pay me thirty and the other go to family. I do paper, and you go."

"Okay, that's fine." Tom sounded surprised at how simple the negotiation for a settlement had been. I pictured Tom reaching into his wallet and handing the policeman $30, which Tom likely took for a service charge, as I did.

The policeman's voice suddenly rose in anger. "No, I want one thousand, and two thousand go to the family."

"I don't have the money with me," Tom said. "It's in our car, and it's too dangerous to go to the car until the morning." I heard the hesitancy in his voice. *He knows something is not right*, I thought.

"It be our secret. Now I go home." I heard feet shuffling. I imagined the policeman's towering shadow on the wall. "I be back at six in the morning to get the money and meet you at eight in my office. I give you paperwork; you go free."

Tom now likely realized that the policeman had asked for 30 percent of the payment of the $3,000 due to the family and had offered us the option of making a run for it. He would return our passports and Cruiser. We could make a dash for the border to get out of Ethiopia and into Sudan, and I would avoid the possible outcome of having to go to prison. Tom returned to our room and closed the heavy door behind him. He sat down on the bed and put his head in his hands.

"I've just agreed to a bribe," he said. "I'm stuck."

"We don't do bribes. You know that." I was too tired to think. My body screamed for sleep.

"Yeah, I know, but I don't know what to do about it now. I misunderstood what he was saying."

"I'm exhausted—we can talk in the morning. Just go to sleep." I closed my eyes to shut out what seemed like just the beginning of an endless nightmare.

Unable to sleep, I tossed in the small squeaking bed, the odors of sweat and tears escaping from the stained gray mattress. And in the darkness, I listened to Tom's breathing. I thought about my childhood and how I used to go to Nanna when I was frightened. She would hold me and say, "You be brave; it's going to be all right. You just stay brave." And in those dark hours, I clung to her words.

The sunlight filtered through the barred windows as roosters crowed, dogs barked, and children laughed and played in the distance—all the universal sounds of a village waking to a new day.

Tom stirred beside me and then sat up with obvious resolve. "I've hardly slept, but I know what I'm going to do now." He left the room and went to sit under a tree.

I swung my legs over the side of the bed. The cement floor felt cold under my feet. I had slept in my dirty clothes, and the smell of my sweat wafted over me. I glanced up at the wall; the gecko was gone. I walked to the doorway and leaned against the frame. A small bent woman approached Tom and offered him coffee. Then a young man appeared near the entrance to the compound and beckoned Tom over. The man seemed nervous. Tom stood up and walked toward him.

"You must be careful," the young man said. "The police are going to try to corrupt you."

"I know," Tom said. "They've already been here. But thank you."

I joined Tom under the tree.

At 6:00 a.m., the policeman arrived and smiled as he greeted us. "Where is my money?" he asked.

Tom stood up. "I don't have it." The strength was back in his voice.

The policeman's eyes burned with rage. "I will see you in the office now." He turned around, walked out through the metal gates of the compound, and disappeared into the small group of locals watching at the entrance.

Once in the office, the policeman indicated, without a word, that we should sit down. I did what I was told, but Tom remained standing.

"You can have your money, but on my conditions," said Tom. His voice was firm yet respectful. His steady eyes fully focused on the policeman, who sat behind the desk. With his right hand open, Tom moved his arm slowly up and down through the air to emphasize his points. "The family still gets their three thousand. Your one thousand will not come out of the family money. It will be a separate payment."

The policeman shrugged. "That be fine."

"My other condition is that there are no secrets, and my wife can take a photo of me giving you the money."

"I can't accept that." The policeman fidgeted with his keychain.

"Why not?" Tom asked.

"Because that is corruption."

"Well, those are my conditions."

"Then I can't help you. You go to Gondar to see the chief of police."

"Must we leave and go to Gondar now?" Tom asked.

"No. Four police will go with you. They will go on the bus, and you must follow the bus. The bus is coming soon. You must go buy their bus tickets."

Tom purchased the tickets for them, but our departure was delayed because the bus hadn't arrived. When we didn't arrive in Gondar as scheduled, the Canadian embassy in Addis Abba called the district chief of police, who then called the local police to ask why we were not yet in Gondar.

Finally, in the late afternoon, we reached our destination, Gondar. Tom arranged for us to stay in a guest room at the Belegez Pension. On our last visit, we had camped in the Belegez parking lot, and the change somehow didn't fit the situation.

I met the district chief of police and our translator, Amanual, a well-built, round-faced young man with a receding hairline and wide eyes who spoke excellent English. After a few awkward moments, I was led into an office and questioned.

Understanding a developing-world judicial system—which included both the official and unofficial systems—as well as the value of a life was complicated. Rules changed; different people came and went. Everything was handwritten on pieces of plain paper. There were no computers, no forms, and no official stamps.

I was so consumed with grief and guilt, struggling endlessly with what had happened, that Tom handled most of the discussions with the officials. I just answered questions directed at me, and then only in as few words as possible.

Amanual explained that if the family agreed, I had the option of negotiating a settlement with them, which would be followed by a traditional trial conducted by the village elders and chiefs. If we failed to come to an agreement, I would have to go to trial through the legal court system.

Tom and I didn't discuss much in the days following the accident except my options. I knew the parents probably would not be able to attend court in Gondor should I choose to go through the legal system. I decided to offer the family the option of negotiating a settlement.

The family accepted my offer to negotiate and agreed that we would attempt to "settle out of court." We arranged to meet the following day, and I couldn't help but feel that the most significant and heartbreaking transaction of my life was about to take place.

Chapter 16
The Power of Forgiveness

Ethiopia, February 2006

Early the following morning, Tom and I entered a large empty room, perhaps a classroom. No officials or police were present. The dead boy's father and two relatives—an uncle and an aunt of the child—along with their negotiator sat across the table from Amanual and us. People outside pressed their noses against the windows to watch. How do you put a price on the life of a little boy? I thought of my sons at the age of nine. They loved soccer. Had Getaw loved soccer? Had he loved running and climbing trees just as my sons had? Had he made his mother laugh at his antics, and had she scolded him when he'd failed to do his homework? What value would I put on the life of my sons? On even the sweet memory of their childhoods? I could hardly breathe for the grief and unrelenting guilt.

The child's father sat still; his eyes focused on his hands, which rested on the table, while his relatives and his negotiator whispered to one another. The negotiator turned and spoke to the father; he then leaned forward and addressed Amanual. Amanual straightened up, shook his head slowly, and replied.

"What did they say?" Tom asked.

Amanual raised his hand toward Tom and said, "Just wait. Still talking."

Wrapped in a cloud of sadness, I blinked back my tears. Words that I could not understand bounced off the gray walls.

Eventually, Amanual turned to Tom and told him what was being said.

Tom tensed up, sighed, and replied, "Tell them it's too much."

I looked up and, through my tears, saw the father staring at me. I now knew his name, Molla. His dark, deep-set eyes fought back the tears. His mouth was small, and when his translator asked him a question, he answered softly in Amharic. I couldn't imagine his pain, no matter how hard I tried.

Amanual shifted in his seat and said to Tom, "They say they want $6,000."

Tom nodded his head. "Okay. That's fine; we'll pay the family."

Nine minutes to negotiate the value of a nine-year-old boy. Sadness consumed me, and I felt disconnected from my thoughts, numbed by grief. I closed my eyes and bowed my head, unable to witness the father's anguish a second longer.

I heard the scraping of chairs, the shuffle of feet, and the murmur of voices.

"They're leaving now, Jan. We can go." Tom touched my shoulder.

I opened my eyes and saw the back of Molla, his head bowed, his shoulders hunched over, as he walked slowly out of the room. Tom reached down and took my hand. "Come. We need to go."

I turned to Amanual and thanked him. He took my hand and said, "You did good. You be okay." But in his eyes, I saw concern. After all, I still had to face the traditional tribal council, which would decide my final fate.

Because we didn't carry enough money with us to pay the family and because the amount we needed was above the limit we could obtain from an ATM, I had no option but to tell my sons about the accident. I picked up the phone and dialed our son in Calgary.

"David, it's Mom." I swallowed hard. "We've had an accident, and I need you to send me some money by tomorrow." I explained some of the details. The anxiety and concern in my son's voice were palpable.

I tried to reassure him. "David, we're okay. I'll be okay. I'll call you again if . . . when we're in Sudan." Doubt and questions about my immediate and long-term fate ground my comforting voice to a whisper.

The following morning, Tom entered the courtyard of the Belegez Pension, where we were staying. "David's emailed. He sent the money. We can withdraw it from the Western Union tomorrow."

At 8:30 the following day, Amanual and Tom returned with the cash—several bundles held together with string in a plain brown paper bag. We immediately proceeded to the office of the chief of police, where I was given two handwritten agreements to sign: one in English, the other in Amharic. Our passports would be returned when payment to the family had been made.

An official dressed in dark pants and with epaulets on his shirt entered the office. He demanded "an agreement from Canada that they will return Janet to Ethiopia at any time we want to question her further."

Tom had finally had enough. He crossed his arms over his chest and spoke firmly. "I'm not prepared to do that. We've signed all the papers, we've met all the conditions, and we need to leave now. You give me our passports. Then and only then will I give the family their money."

The official stood up, eyes flaring, and waved his fist at Tom. "The embassy must send a letter. Janet must come back to Ethiopia if we need to question her more."

"The embassy will not send a letter. Give me our passports now." Tom's grip tightened on the paper bag.

The tension rose like heat in the room. We were in standoff mode, with Tom and the official raising their voices, haggling, and arguing. A group of policemen and locals gathered in the doorway. The official left the office. He said he would phone the embassy himself and demand a letter. My life suddenly appeared to unravel before me. My fate lay entirely in the hands of strangers. I was trapped between different cultures, values, beliefs, languages, and legal systems.

"Let's get out of here," said Tom. We walked out of the office and into the parking lot.

Without saying a word, we knew we needed some privacy and a break from the tension. So, we sat in our vehicle. It was now ten in the morning. We had to leave Gondar by midday because a Land Cruiser had been booked for the police to escort us to the child's village, where I was scheduled to stand trial that afternoon. The money was the only bargaining chip we had. We knew that as soon as we handed the money over, we would have no more power. The father, meanwhile, was also tired and wanted to leave.

We watched in silence through our dusty windshield as the scene unfolded before us. Men came and went, some in uniform and some dressed casually. They huddled in groups and then approached the family, who stood in the shade of the wall.

Amanual walked toward us. "I need some of the money," he said urgently.

Tom reached into the bag and handed him a small amount of cash. Stray dogs barked in the distance; more locals arrived. Several payments were made between our translator, the father, and the police. Amanual again asked for some money. With only thirty minutes to go before we had to leave, Tom went to look for the chief of police. No letter had arrived from the embassy.

Feeling desperate, Tom asked, "What can we do to solve this problem?"

"If the embassy won't send a letter, then the Canada government must give Janet diplomatic immunity," the chief said. "Then I give you the passports, and you go."

Tom called the Canadian embassy. The person who answered the phone said, "I have no idea what they mean by diplomatic immunity but tell them Janet has it."

The chief of police returned our passports. Tom handed the bag of cash to the father, and we left Gondar for the boy's village under an armed police escort. There I would face the child's mother and the village elders. But it was only Getaw's mother I thought about.

The village was about a four-hour drive from Gondar. Tom drove. I looked out the window, beyond the fields of yellow teff, past the horizon, to the end of the world. I saw men and women beside the road. I especially noticed the children on the sides of the road, and I dared not think about how my day might end.

Finally, we arrived at the turnoff to the village. There was no road, only a bush track through the tall grass. The police parked their car on the roadside and walked with rifles at the ready beside us as Tom drove through the bush toward the village. The villagers sat waiting for us on rows of wooden benches beneath a majestic, widely spread tree with dark leaves. We were greeted with wails and cries.

Tom took my hand and squeezed it. He leaned over and whispered, "Just keep doing the right thing, and it will be okay."

I noticed a pretty young woman weeping softly into a little pair of boy's brown pants, which she clutched tightly to her breasts. Several strands of black leather were wrapped around her wrists. She wore a long skirt with tiny flowers and a loose, light gray plain top. Her soft dark hair was braided with small colorful beads. She walked slowly toward me, stirring the dust beneath her sandaled feet. *She must be the mother. It must be Enatelem,* I thought. We looked at each other in silence and gently shook hands. Her hand was sweaty, her large brown eyes swollen beneath her long eyelashes and her flawless complexion glistened with tears in the sunlight.

They directed Tom and me to sit on a bench alongside the family. I sat beside the mother, who whimpered into the little boy's shorts. A small toddler clung to her skirt and cried. My heart seemed to stop beating, and then it felt as if it beat inside my temples and all through my limbs. None of my senses were familiar to me. I looked around almost without sensation. Nothing could have prepared me for this moment.

Several village elders, the policemen, and the father stood before the villagers. An older man with silver streaks through his dark hair spoke with authority in his voice to the crowd. I assumed he was the village chief, partly because he was a large man and towered over the father, who stood slightly behind him. Holding a stick in his right hand, the chief pointed at the policeman when he had finished speaking.

The policeman spoke. I couldn't understand, but the villagers and officials seemed to be asking questions and exchanging information. I felt the mother tremble beside me, but I couldn't reach out to comfort her.

Amanual turned to me. "The village chief and the people want you to say something."

I stood up. Choking back my tears, I expressed my sorrow at what had happened. "What happened to Getaw was a tragedy." I struggled to find the right words. "As a mother of two children, of two sons, I cannot imagine the pain his parents must be experiencing." My voice trembled, and words seemed trapped in my throat. "I am so sorry about the accident. Tom and I wanted to honor little Getaw's life, and I hope we have done that." I no longer recognized my voice. "I also want to thank everyone who helped us during this difficult time." I looked at the father, and then I turned to the mother beside me. "I am so sorry," I whispered. Grief and guilt had crushed me. I sat back down beside Getaw's mother, and her sobs drowned what was left of my strength.

The policeman translated my words, and more discussion among the villagers ensued. Finally, the policeman turned to me. "The villagers say they know it was an accident and that you should not cry for the boy."

Amanual walked over to me. "You are free to go."

Suddenly, just like that, I was free. The reality was too much to take in at first. Even though my body still shook, I finally noticed my breathing again.

As Tom and I stood up to go, the mother approached me. Through Amanual, she thanked me for stopping, for rendering first aid and taking her son to a clinic, and for trying to save her child's life. We stood together, two mothers enveloped in grief. She stepped forward and embraced me. As we held each other and cried, I entered another zone of existence. Her pain and grief soaked through me, and it was as if we had become one mother. It flashed through my mind that she would never hug her son again. When we clung to each other, I was so close to her, her breath became my breath, and I felt as if my own child had died. Sensing her tender forgiveness, I wept even more.

The child's family invited us for a coffee ceremony in honor of Getaw's life. Tom and I knew what a privilege it was to be invited to this special event. As parents who had raised sons together, we looked at each other and bowed our heads in respect. Tom gratefully accepted their invitation.

We entered their small mud hut. A little girl of about eighteen months sat on the dirt floor. Rolled-up bedding was stacked to the side, and Getaw's clothing still hung from a peg on the wall. Chickens scratched the ground in the doorway. I sat on the floor and held the cup of coffee between my hands. Tom put his arm around my shoulder and whispered in my ear, "We're both here, but you're doing the hard work; you're getting us through it."

The setting sun had sunk almost below the horizon by the time the police finally escorted us to the Sudan border, where we bade them farewell and thanked them for their support.

I turned to Amanual. He smiled and took my hand. "You should not feel sad. By this time next year, she will have another. Children die all the time."

Every part of me wanted to loudly announce Getaw's uniqueness to the heavens, to acknowledge the specific pain that his mother could never feel again, no matter how many children she lost. In this regard, Getaw's mother and I perhaps stood apart from the men of any race. Though I knew that Tom also suffered on behalf of the Ethiopian family, that he could never take such a cavalier view of life and death (because he'd never had to learn to do so), I also knew that the mother's embrace contained a kind of gentle keening borne of motherhood's hope and pain.

As Tom and I drove slowly into our resurrected freedom, Ethiopia began to fade behind us. I felt a tightening of all my muscles, as if my whole being had been imprisoned rather than released. I couldn't help but wonder if I had crossed over a different kind of border—of pain, loss, tragic understanding—from which I might never be able to turn back to the known and familiar. And if that were the case, could Tom even come with me? Even more than before the accident, our journey now seemed tenuous and fraught with an underlying tension that we still hadn't fully addressed.

Ahead of us lay a tragic, war-torn country; it seemed only fitting to enter it with a mother's tears still on my skin and the weight of salt heavy on my tongue.

Chapter 17
Would I Ever Find Peace Again?

Sudan, March 2006

The Sudanese border-control policeman lifted the boom across the road, and we crossed out of Ethiopia into Sudan. Tom parked the Cruiser in the late-afternoon shadow of the compound wall. We got out and walked across the parking lot to the Immigration and Customs complex. An imposing man wearing an ankle-length dark-purple *jalabiyya*—a robe with long sleeves—approached us. The equally dark-purple turban he wore made him look seven feet tall. He had a broad face with piercing brown eyes.

Tom handed him our passports. Without looking at them, the official asked, "You from Denmark?" The booming tone of his voice sounded accusatory and threatening.

Tom shook his head. "No, sir. You have our Canadian passports in your hand."

The large man waved our passports in the air. "Good answer. No Danish people allowed!"

I had forgotten about the Danish-cartoons that offensively depicted the Prophet Mohammed and had resulted in violent protests and riots across the Muslim world. That controversy seemed so long ago, although it had been only ten days since we had removed the Canadian flag from our car, afraid that its colors would be confused with those of a Danish flag. A flutter of anxiety swept through me.

"What do you think of the Darfur crisis?" the official asked.

Oh, God, I thought, *the war*. In all the recent grief and stress, I had forgotten about the Darfur conflict in Sudan. We wouldn't be going near the Darfur region, but I knew that events in a destabilized nation could change in an instant. Was there anything happening in Sudan that we didn't know about but should?

Tom hesitated slightly before replying, "I don't know, sir. I've only just arrived in your country."

"I tell you the problem," the official scowled. "Too many foreign armies."

"I agree, sir," said Tom. "There are too many foreign armies in Sudan."

The official stamped our documents. We returned to our car. Tom got out our satellite phone, and I called home.

David answered. I heard myself say, "We're safely in Sudan."

Just hearing my son's relief over the phone from thousands of miles away helped to soothe my nerves. With the resulting calm and the knowledge that the horrible days were finally behind us, I had, at last, an opportunity to reflect on all I'd learned about my native continent and myself on this trip.

I knew that I'd always be a traveler on this continent. Even though I was born and raised here, I simply couldn't escape my unease long enough to truly experience the pressing weight of history all around me, the weight that is so crushing to millions. Not for the first or last time, I vowed to pay closer and more thoughtful attention to the realities of the continent I only ever knew in glimpses. But often, the sheer demands of travel—nightmarish at times—forced us to consider only the immediate challenges and not the broader picture. And now, I wondered if I would ever be able to see anything again except that little boy's terrified face sinking under the front of our Cruiser. At that moment, I seriously doubted it, nor was I sure I even had the moral right to see and enjoy the Africa I had wanted so much to find again. But then, the pain was raw, and I couldn't foresee at the time that my honoring of Africa in all its stunning variety, the darkness included, was also a form of genuine remembrance for the death I'd caused.

The night descended and tossed a million stars into the sky. Tom set up camp outside the Sudan-police border-control compound. Truckers settled down to wait for the border to open in the morning. They sat around charcoal fires, laughing and chatting in Arabic or Amharic, and the comforting aroma of cooking goat meat drifted toward our camp. Some men rolled out prayer rugs and, facing Mecca, knelt and bowed down to pray. Others prepared their beds beneath their trucks. The scene appeared peaceful, although I couldn't find any peace in it. I wondered if I could ever find peace again.

Tom joined me as I sat on the tailgate of our Land Cruiser and put his arm around my shoulders. I felt chilled in the warm evening air and leaned into his warmth. We'd been pushed into survival mode—with events moving so quickly, we'd had to make decisions with mere glances, touches, and a few words—and we'd relied on each other to make the right choices without questions. We had shared fear and courage, despair and hope, but it was as if we couldn't put the emotions into language. Even so, Tom had stood beside me, close and yet apart; his compassionate strength became my strength. He understood my need to take full responsibility for the horrific accident and to accept the consequences. And in those moments, I knew our relationship had reached a level of trust and intimacy I had never felt before.

Exhausted, unwashed, and sweating, I entered our tent and crawled into bed. Eventually, I fell asleep, but the haunting voices of the night woke me, and I lay in the dark, trembling with fear. As the sun rose, I heard the mullah calling the faithful to prayer. Above his melodic chant, the donkeys brayed, the dogs barked, and I wept with sorrow, but now, also with relief. I was safely in Sudan, and the possibility of imprisonment was gone. It would take some time, however, and rightly so, for my spirit and my nature to recover their characteristic freedom.

Tom, meanwhile, was eager to reach Khartoum, the capital, that day. He climbed hurriedly out of the tent to make coffee. When he got down to the ground, I heard his agitated cry. "There's damn oil leaking from the rear diff. We've got a serious problem."

I closed my eyes, wanting to shut out the world. Was this a serious problem? How could anything be a serious problem after what we'd just been through? Tom climbed up to the tent to explain that we would need to make it to Gedaref (Al Qadarif) and hopefully get the Cruiser repaired there. He tugged at my toes. "You need to get up. We've got to go. We've a hundred miles of terrible road ahead."

Robotically, I forced myself to reenter the quotidian world of travel and destinations and practical choices. Perhaps, I thought, the drive would distract me from my relentless guilt.

The road was as bad as rumored—a gravel road that at times disappeared as if swallowed by the desert. Tom was nervous that we wouldn't complete this leg of the trip before the differential ran dry and seized, and I tried to participate in his concern. All around us, the world was scorched brown and desolate. Dirty clouds of dust boiled against the receding horizon. The sky ahead was endless. I felt alone and isolated from the world. Tom stopped every half hour to check if we still had oil leaking from the differential; if so, we were okay. With each stop, I waited to hear, "We're still good," but I didn't much care either way. I felt as fragile as our differential. Would I even make it to Cairo?

Six hours later, Gedaref appeared on the horizon like a mirage, a dusty haze of buildings. Tom pulled into a gas station on the outskirts of town. Ten minutes later, we entered the lobby of the first hotel we came across, and Tom asked where we could eat. A man waved us to a stark, empty eating area. Tom ordered the third item on the menu, which was written in Arabic. My stomach heaved at the sight of the food.

"I can't eat." I put my hand over my mouth and waited.

Tom waved the flies away from his food. "You're pale, and you look terrible. I'll see if we can get a room. You can sleep. I'll go and see if I can get the Cruiser fixed."

Before long, Tom led me to the small room he'd rented, and I lay down on the bed. The yellow walls crowded in on me as the room swayed. Noises from the passageway roared through my head, and my body throbbed. I closed my eyes. I felt things crawl over my sweaty body. I tried in vain to wipe them away. I got up to get a bucket from the toilet and returned to the bed. I sat on the bed, pulled my knees toward my chest, and placed the bucket between my knees. My stomach revolted. I watched the fleas eating me alive and sucking me dry. The hours passed; night fell and stole the light from the room. I heard the child's voice, his pitiful cry, and I reached out to hold him.

"He's gone, he's gone," I sobbed.

At some point—it must have been hours later—Tom walked into the room.

"The Cruiser's fixed . . . Jesus Christ, you look like hell. What happened?" He grabbed me by both shoulders. "You're covered in fleas. Why didn't you get another room?"

I couldn't speak. I could barely even lift my head.

"I'll be right back." He hurried away to the front desk.

Ten minutes later, once we had settled into a new room, Tom helped me step out of my clothes and into a small tin basin. He scooped up a cup of cold water from a bucket and washed the fleas from my naked body. His rough hands lathered me with cheap carbolic soap. The acidic vinegar smell of the soap stung my nostrils.

Cold water ran down my sides. I shivered. Tom opened the window above the bed, and the warm night air soothed my aching body. He took my arms and helped me step out of the basin. My wet hair dripped water down my back. Tom hugged me close to his warm body. "I'm so sorry I left you," he said. "I didn't realize you were in such a bad state." I abandoned myself in his arms and closed my eyes. "I'm tired," I whispered.

I lay down on the thin gray sheet covering the single iron-framed bed pushed up against the wall. Tom sat on the bed opposite. I closed my eyes. In the distance, the mullah's call from the mosque, similar to a Gregorian chant, lulled me to sleep.

I woke to the sun streaming through the window, my body covered in angry red fleabites. I splashed cold water onto my face, all the while knowing I still lacked any appetite. I would have to endure our long day ahead on an empty stomach. It was 250 miles to Khartoum. The prospect of the journey was deadening.

Tom reorganized our Cruiser and made a place for me to lie down. I curled up and drifted back to a fitful sleep. About an hour later, several men's voices woke me. Tom had been stopped at a military checkpoint and was speaking to at least three armed men in uniforms.

Tom turned around to speak to me. "We've got to register and give them our exact route to Khartoum. You stay in the car; I'll do it." He got out, and I watched the soldiers talking to him. They had our passports and were stamping and writing something into them. Then they waved him goodbye, and Tom returned to the car.

"They've registered us and the route we're taking," Tom said. "We can't deviate from it. They'll be watching and checking that we stay on our route."

I lay back down, just wanting the day to end.

In the late afternoon, we entered Khartoum, a large modern city of five million. A dusty haze hung over the chaotic dance of cars, buses, trucks, and pedestrians as everyone tried to weave their way through the bustling city—a city rich from oil and gas revenues.

We made our way to the National Camp Site, located in a military complex, and parked in the sandy parking lot. The hundred-degree heat hit me as I stepped out of the Cruiser. Tom wandered off to find a tap. I sat down on the dusty red gravel and leaned against a palm tree. Like the tree, I felt rooted to the earth.

Tom returned, calling, "Look who's here." He pointed to two travelers, Alison and David, whom we'd met in Nairobi. They greeted me with cheerful smiles and hugs. It felt good to be with friends again, and I was briefly hopeful that the feeling would begin to rouse me from my torpor of grief.

They invited us to join them for the evening and asked how long we planned to be in Khartoum. We hadn't planned to stay long, but with the thought of heading off again, a heavy sense of weariness lodged in me.

The night was still warm. David stoked the glowing embers of the small fire with a stick, careful not to touch a battered silver pot dangling from a pole. From out of it, Alison offered us sweet black tea and juicy dates covered in coconut flakes.

I pulled up my legs and held my cup between my hands in front of my knees. Alison sat cross-legged on the ground beside the campfire. Tom, beside me, stretched out his legs and leaned back on his hands. With his wild beard, tired eyes, and deeply tanned muscular arms and legs, he appeared scarred by our recent experiences. I was surprised by, and unprepared for, how much older he suddenly looked.

That evening around their campfire, I told our friends about the accident in Ethiopia. From a very great distance, I listened to my quivering voice telling the whole story for the first time, and my body heaved with sobs. There were tears for the child, for his mother and father, and for Tom and me. Yet slowly, out of the chaos of my wounded psyche, I had taken the first step out of the nightmare; there would be many more, just as faltering, to come, but at least I had started the journey, a much deeper and more meaningful parallel to the mere physical adventure I had once imagined would change my reality.

Without turning his head, Tom glanced sideways at me, his eyes watching my lips. I saw a glint of a tear roll down the side of his nose. He reached up and brushed the wetness away.

Alison grasped my arm, crying. David expressed his shock and disbelief. In a halting voice, he asked Tom, "And how are you doing?"

In a barely heard whisper, Tom said, "I'm just starting to real-ize everything we went through." His chest heaved. "The thought of Jan going to prison was absolutely unbearable . . . I was terrified I was going to lose her." His lips began to tremble. He leaned over and pulled me fiercely into his arms. "Thank God you didn't go to prison."

I fought back that nightmarish thought and clung to Tom as fiercely as he clung to me. Like silent ghosts, the smell of sweat, dust, and smoke lingered over us. I murmured, as though announcing the fact to myself, "It's over, Tom, it's over." A stillness descended over the surrounding darkness, and it wasn't long before we all said good night. Tom and I returned to our tent, agreeing to spend several days resting in Khartoum.

The following morning, we wandered, lost in our thoughts, through the bustling city streets—men dressed in suits mingled with men dressed in traditional loose-fitting white robes. Noisy children with colorful school backpacks jostled one another with joy and warmth. During the heat of the day, I lay in the shade of palm trees, watching flocks of blackbirds soar above. Later Tom joined me, and we watched a plane fly high overhead, leaving an evanescent trail of its journey in a cloudless blue sky. For a moment, I wished I was on that plane. But we had agreed it would be quicker to drive across Sudan to Egypt than to arrange to ship our vehicle from Port Sudan.

Until now, we hadn't been able to talk about the accident at length. I had been shocked the night before when Tom expressed how fearful he had been, how terrified he was at the thought that I might go to prison. In my grief and despair following the accident, I had never once asked him how he was doing. Perhaps, I thought, this failure pointed to some genuine barrier in our relationship; probably, there had always been some level of communication we couldn't reach together.

I pulled myself into a sitting position and gazed at Tom's curiously unfamiliar profile. How well did I really know him? Haltingly, I spoke. "I'm so sorry. About after the accident, I mean. I was so consumed by my suffering that I never asked you how you were doing." I waited a few seconds as his profile disappeared, and I saw his broad, enquiring face, almost familiar again. "So, tell me, how *are* you truly doing?"

Tom sat still, hardly seeming to breathe. I grew anxious and tried to read his thoughts. Reaching out and taking his hand, I felt the roughness of his fingers against my skin.

"I'm okay now," he said. "But I'd never known such fear. After the accident . . ." Beads of sweat ran down the side of his face. "I knew I had to manage it, but I had no idea how."

A military vehicle angrily kicked up dust and small stones as it passed. Tom looked at me and then down at the ground. I felt my world pause as I waited for him to speak again.

Tom looked up. "But after the police accepted that I wasn't open to bribes, I felt some hope." He stared out across the compound, his brown eyes squinting in the sun, his lips puckered tightly together. Then he relaxed his mouth and released a loud sigh. "I had an 'Oh fuck' moment," he said, "when the police wanted that letter from the embassy agreeing that you'd return to Ethiopia if the police demanded it. But that was also a turning point for me. I knew then that I had to stand my ground."

As if coming out of a coma, I began to realize what Tom had gone through. All along, I had just assumed that he was coping. I had no idea what thoughts or emotions were behind his actions. My suffering had blinded me to his experience, and I wondered how often that had been the case. We each had to examine our roles in the breakdown of our marriage.

"I'm so sorry I put you through all that." Regret gnawed right down to my marrow.

"Don't apologize. You had plenty to deal with yourself. Anyway, we were in it together. We both had to pull on our strength to get through."

Tom's shoulders dropped as his tense muscles eased. We both agreed that the empathy and compassion shown by the nurse, the translator, the locals, and even the police had helped us cope.

"During the village trial," Tom said, "I felt I was somewhere else, like I was watching a movie. Getting out of Ethiopia before the border closed at 5:00 p.m. was all I could focus on."

"When Getaw's mother held me," I said, "I thought . . . I thought I would break."

Tom listened quietly.

"I needed someone to tell me everything would be okay, and it was her, she told me—not in words, but with her sobs, tears, and her body pressed against mine."

A breeze stirred the dust, and a plastic bag rolled by.

"We'll be okay," Tom said. I heard the truth of his statement in the conviction in his voice, which I knew rose out of a genuine belief in our relationship.

Over the next few days, more travelers arrived at the campsite, including a young couple, Marc and Maria, who wanted someone to convoy with them north to Egypt. An exhausted Dutch motorcyclist also arrived after completing the grueling five-day ride from Wadi Halfa. He rode into the camp and collapsed onto the dirt ground. As he lay there, spread-eagle, he admitted he'd badly underestimated how challenging the ride would be. He later commiserated with a biker from New Zealand who was trying to repair his bike's suspension. It had blown up on the same track, forcing him to hitch a ride on a Sudanese truck.

In the evenings, everyone debated which route to take across the Sahara. Tom and I had decided to follow the Nile River to the village of Wadi Halfa on Lake Nubia, the Sudanese section of Lake Nasser.

No foreigners were permitted to drive between the two countries, apparently because of land mines buried along the border. So, from the village of Wadi Halfa, we'd have to take a three-day ferry trip down the lake to the port city of Aswan in Egypt.

Marc and Maria agreed to convoy with us on the challenging several-day drive across the Sahara. We would face terrific heat and isolation. The prospect was unnerving, but I hoped we were ready for whatever the desert would throw at us. Before leaving the city, Tom needed to replace the air conditioner fan belt. Marc said they would follow us to the Toyota dealer, and from there, we would all head north.

In a maze of traffic and alleyways, we lost sight of them. Suddenly we found ourselves stuck in the middle of a raucous protest. Police had moved in and blocked off the streets. We could not understand what was happening or what the police were shouting. But somehow, we had managed to slip past the police barriers. Before we knew it, a crowd of thousands of marchers, mostly men, waving banners and shouting in Arabic, surrounded us. "Allah Akbar," they yelled. Some wore regular slacks and shirts, while others wore traditional white robes. We had no idea what the angry protest was about. We were the only foreigners, and the only other vehicles in sight were police vehicles.

"Open your window," Tom said. "Try to look friendly."

I rolled down my window, and people immediately thrust their arms inside. "Allah Akbar," they said and shook my hand. Unsure what to do or say, I simply returned the greeting.

Tom and I speculated on the possible reason for the protest.

"Do you think it's about the cartoons?" I asked.

"I don't know, but if it is, thank God we took the Canadian flag off our car."

Trapped in the turmoil, we were swept along for several hours before we could finally escape the mass of humanity.

We made our way to the Toyota dealer, and the mechanics replaced the air conditioner fan belt. But because it was late, we returned to the campsite for the night. Marc and Maria were not at the camp, and we had no idea what had happened to them. However, Tom and I agreed we would leave Khartoum in the morning regardless. We just hoped they had made it out of the city and were waiting for us to catch up with them.

Getting out of Khartoum in the morning was a logistical nightmare. The city center was completely choked with traffic, more protestors, and police, and nothing moved. The large protest continued—we later learned it was about the UN presence in the Darfur war in western Sudan—which had turned the city streets into a raging, noisy, giant parking lot. As the only foreign-looking people in the crowd, we weren't comfortable about our presence. It therefore came as a considerable relief when, after two hours, we found ourselves swept toward the outskirts of the city and the Nile River. With gratitude, we drove across the White Nile Bridge and into the ancient city of Omdurman.

The second-largest city in Sudan, Omdurman lies on the western banks of the Nile River opposite Khartoum. It is best known as the cultural capital of Sudan, with the National Theatre and puppet theaters, prominent poets and writers, gifted musicians, and the mystical whirling dervishes. But art and music weren't foremost in our minds, as we had the usual confounding cityscape to figure out first. We struggled to navigate through a chaotic maze of narrow and crooked ancient single-lane streets and alleyways that weaved around souks, mosques, barbershops, butchers, fish and vegetable stalls, and houses. Eventually, we were staring down a narrow strip of tarmac road that sliced the red Bayuda Desert sands in half for as far as our eyes could see. Finally, we entered the desert, heading north toward Wadi Halfa, 640 miles away.

Four hours later, the road degenerated into a corrugated and potholed track. Soon after, we watched a haboob—a sandstorm—blast across the sandy emptiness toward us. The world disappeared, and the dust storm swallowed us up. We couldn't even see the front of our vehicle.

"This is not good," I said.

Tom shook his head. "We could be stuck here—or worse, buried here and never found."

Our only option was to wait. The sun disappeared, and darkness engulfed us. Rushing, angry brown sand howled around the car, and I wondered whether we would even make it to Egypt.

The storm was still blowing the next morning when Tom noticed brake fluid leaking from the rear left wheel, the same brake he'd had fixed in Zambia. We were alone in a desolate, barren landscape, miles from any garage.

"We'll just have to drive slowly and carefully," Tom said, "and only use the brake if essential."

Petrified at the thought of driving through a village with poor brakes, I said I didn't know if I could do it.

"I'll drive really slowly. And the deep sand will also slow us down. I'll get it fixed in Dongola. It's not too far now."

I knew I had no other option but to agree to continue. It was the same option—only in physical terms—of what my spirit had faced and still faced in the wake of the child's death. In a way, the sandstorm almost seemed to enclose us for a reason, so that we could enter the world again, our vision a little clearer but our transit still heavy and damaged. Though I could see the way ahead now, I wondered where it was that I hoped to arrive in and whether I would get there.

Chapter 18

I Am Because of You

Sudan, March 2006

We set off early for the town of Dongola, located on the banks of the Nile. We hadn't gone far when Tom pointed to a cloud of dust in the distance on the dirt road ahead.

"That's them," he yelled. Within several minutes, we pulled alongside Marc and Maria. Tom rolled down his window and asked why they were going so slowly. Marc said the deplorable road conditions had broken their truck's suspension. They couldn't go any faster than twelve miles an hour. Although relieved that we were no longer tackling another vehicle-wrecking leg of the journey alone, I remained troubled about the road, which was reputed to have the worst corrugations in the world. Tom later abandoned the corrugated track and drove off-road across the softer desert sand.

Several hours later, we all arrived in Dongola. From here, we would make the short ferry ride across the Nile. At the loading area on the banks of the river, Tom parked behind the lineup of heavily loaded white Toyota pickup trucks, a tanker with "Alasfia Petroleum" written on the side, and a gaily painted yellow bus, its roof overloaded with bags of goods, bales of wood, bicycles, and barrels of cooking oil.

Tom got out of the Cruiser and approached an older man squatting on his haunches in the shade of a small blue wood shack with a bamboo roof. He asked where he could find a mechanic. The gray-haired man in a traditional white robe smiled and stood up. Waving his right arm, he yelled in Arabic to a group of young men standing

201

beside the rusted skeleton of an abandoned yellow bulldozer. One of these young men—wearing an open-neck shirt, long brown pants, and sandals—strode toward Tom and greeted him with a broad smile that revealed his perfect white teeth.

"Car broke?" he asked.

Tom tried to explain, using gestures and pointing to the brakes, that he needed a mechanic. The young man's English appeared to be limited to about twenty words. Exasperated by his failure to get his point across, Tom turned to me and asked, "I don't suppose you know the Arabic word for 'mechanic'?"

Finally, after much gesturing, Tom had some success, and three men arrived, all wearing grease- and oil-stained clothing and each with a spanner in his hand. But we already had spanners. Unfortunately, it appeared likely that our Cruiser, with its failing brakes, and Marc's truck, with its broken suspension, would have to limp into Egypt.

"*Inshallah*. God willing," I whispered. All I had left in me was the hope we would make it safely.

Seeking some shade while waiting for the ferry, I wandered off. Wisps of white clouds in the hazy pale-blue sky above taunted the parched earth and the sweaty people below. Two light-brown one-hump camels—both had one front leg tied up so they couldn't run—seemed oblivious to the heat. Their large dark eyes with impressive long eyelashes watched me walk their way, but their groan-like grunts made me take a wide berth around them.

Scrawny chickens, some with their legs tied together, waited in cages made of sticks and ropes. A gray burlap cloth had been thrown over the cages to shade them. Some chickens squawked, and the smell of chicken shit wafted over the cages. Suddenly, there was a commotion, and an escaped bird screeched and flapped its wings as several excited young boys chased after it. The luckless fowl never stood a chance. Before too long, a grinning youngster returned, holding the chicken upside down at his side. Gray feathers swirled around in the wind.

As I watched the numerous rickety, overloaded passenger ferries and colorful fishing boats plying the brown river, I tried to push the accident out of my mind. I still couldn't fathom what Tom and I had gone through. Horribly and unremittingly real as it was, the whole event nevertheless seemed to exist in some other world, some other time. In a daze, I wandered down to the river's edge, where small boats lay haphazardly arranged on the shore. A young man, sitting beside a small blue rowboat mending a black fishing net, looked up and nodded at me but said nothing. Then I felt a hand on my shoulder and turned around.

"Come, Jan," Tom said. "We need to go back to the car. They're going to start loading soon."

"But what about the brakes?" I asked. The risks of driving with poor brakes, especially through the villages, terrified me.

"We'll be fine. When I take my foot off the accelerator, I just sink into the sand. Besides, we've only got 310 miles to go."

A small boy startled me when he burst from between two boats holding up a silverfish. He sported a boyish grin as he showed the fish to the young man mending the net.

The barefoot boy, with mud up to his skinny knees, looked up at me, his dark eyes full of innocence and wonder. Almost at once, he giggled and wiggled his fish in the air for me to see.

I gasped for breath. *He's about the same age, the same size*, I thought, and an overwhelming desire to hold the child surged through me.

Tom's voice cut through my silent thoughts. "The Cruiser has backup brakes, and if I go really slowly in the villages, we'll be okay." He took my hand. "Come. We need to go."

His hand was sticky and hot, and I pulled away. "You go. I'll be right there. Just give me a moment." As if trapped in time, I stood still and watched the child, my mouth dry. I brushed away tears.

I don't know how long it was before I heard Tom's urgent call. "Jan. Come on! We're leaving."

I turned and slowly walked back to the Cruiser. Some men knelt in prayer on the sandy banks before boarding the ferry, and I hoped the prayers weren't related to the river crossing.

Diesel fumes puffed into the air as vehicle engines started up. Tom drove onto the brightly colored blue-and-green rickety ferry loaded with trucks, camels, chickens, and goats. Locals greeted us with friendly smiles and called out, "*Ahlaan bik*," welcome. The stench of sweat, incense, fish, diesel, and unwashed animals hardly seemed noticed by the noisy crowd cramped onboard. The wind caused little whitecaps to appear on the waves of the brown water. But the men standing or sitting on the tops of vehicles or the gunwales of the ferry seemed utterly tranquil. I stared at the water. The vast and mighty Nile River, the longest river in the world (at 4,260 miles), supports many villages and communities along its journey to the Mediterranean Sea. I had a sense of privilege as we ferried across this waterway of ancient wars, peace, and life itself—floating on history, on a ribbon of life in the middle of a sea of sand.

The day after the ferry crossing, we stopped at a little village, and within minutes of our arrival, barefoot children rushed out to greet us. We parked next to the tap, but we needed to find the keeper of the tap so we could obtain permission to get water. Several women emerged from their homes as a young boy set off running to find the keeper of the tap. A plump middle-aged woman approached me and indicated for me to follow her. Her smile radiated warmth. Tom said he would wait for the keeper to arrive.

The woman and I walked into the village, and she stopped beside a shelter—two walls supporting a roof of palm leaves. In the shade of the palm leaves stood two large limestone pots with a thin film of green moss growing around the bottom. Drops of water slowly leaked through the limestone, and the constant breeze kept the drinking water inside the pots cool. The woman reached for a ladle and showed me how to fill my water bottle. While I did so, the aroma of freshly baked bread drifted over us, and I indicated to the woman that I would also like to buy bread. "*Khabaz*," I said. "Bread." The woman led me down the alley, and I purchased three loaves of round flatbread, the size of small pizzas, before returning to Tom.

When I arrived, I saw four scruffy, dusty children had surrounded Tom. A friendly middle-aged man, the keeper of the tap, stood by and watched Tom fill the water tanks in our vehicle. An older man dressed in traditional white robes sat on a mound of black rocks, quietly watching the scene below while swatting mosquitoes. Once the keeper of the tap was reassured that we had sufficient water, he waved us on.

Because it was late in the day, we decided to stay near the village. We set up camp among the palm trees heavily laden with dates and the scrubby acacia desert shrubs that lined the banks of the Nile. Hundreds of mosquitoes joined us.

I woke at dawn to the new sound of the continuous *phut-phut-phut* of creaking water pumps and the familiar croaking of frogs in the distance. The first soft light of the day filtered in through the opened tent door, and the aroma of freshly brewed coffee invited me to get up and join the rest of the early morning campers. Everyone was eager to get going before the heat of midday.

I could hear village fishermen on the river, and I thought of the keeper of the tap, the children, and the woman who had helped me find fresh drinking water and freshly baked bread the day before. Their concern for our well-being and safety helped me in my struggles to stay focused on getting to Cairo safely.

For the next four days, we bounced, rattled, and jarred our way north through the desert, hordes of flies our constant companions. At times, we hugged the riverbank, and at other times we veered so far east that the river wasn't visible. In villages, the road sliced the desert in two: harsh, sandy, and barren on one side and lush green fields of wheat, fodder, and other crops watered by the Nile on the other. Life and death gazing into each other's faces.

The Nubian villages on the banks of the Nile are enclosed by tall brick walls that offer protection against blowing sand and heat. The villages seemed strangely deserted because the inhabitants live mostly closeted in their courtyards. Living on the edge of life, they understand better than anyone the risks and dangers of traveling across deserts.

The challenging drive across the desolate and forgotten world of windswept dunes and hot black rocks seemed endless. The corrugations threatened to shake loose every bolt on the Cruiser. Between the corrugated portions, the track was either covered by deep, soft sand or sharp, rocky scree. It required the driver's constant attention and was slow going. Driving twelve to fourteen hours a day, we could only do about fifty to sixty miles. At times the Cruiser would suddenly drop into a hole filled with dust as fine as talcum powder. We couldn't see these depressions, and because the dust couldn't support the weight of the vehicle, we sank like a stone into it. A film of dust covered everything, a film we designated as "clean dirt" and edible because it was easier to eat it than to get it out of our food.

Often when we stopped to rest, curious Sudanese children would sit quietly around us, observing our every move, and then slip away as if they'd been a mirage, leaving only their little footprints in the sand. These children asked for nothing more from us than friendship.

Once as they walked away, a little boy turned around, smiled, and waved goodbye to me, his eyes alive with joy. *He looks about the same age*, I thought. I smiled and waved back, but a torrent of guilt and sadness tore through me. I looked away and then walked over a large dune and into loneliness.

We camped among the silent dunes, and the clear night skies filled with infinite sparkling stars, the planets, and the moon. I watched the crimson sunsets and woke to the gentle dawns. In the evenings, when we camped on the banks of the Nile, the Sudanese fishermen brought us fresh fish. "*Shukraan*," Tom would say, thanking them, and then he'd add, "Please, we'd like to pay you or give you something." But we were always told, "No, you are guests in our country."

They had so little and yet offered us so much. I struggled every day and, at times, even wondered whether the tragedy would always haunt me or whether, eventually, I would find peace. A gentleness had evolved between Tom and me since the accident. *Perhaps*, I thought, *our renewed relationship is the beginning of finding peace.*

By day five, exhaustion had set in, to the point where even my unwashed body, covered in dust and sweat, no longer mattered. In the scorching heat, I watched restless grains of sand dance in the ceaseless wind that blew among the dunes. In the emptiness of the desert, my life felt as insignificant as a grain of sand.

Finally, after six days of rough desert traveling, the blue waters of Lake Nubia came into view. The sight of so much fresh water in the desert, with not even a blade of grass at the lake's edge, took my breath away. The original village of Wadi Halfa had been flooded during the building of the Aswan Dam. The new village, located farther away from the lake, was a cluster of run-down shacks built by people forgotten by the world. The shamble of open-air, plastic-covered stalls sold food and other goods to travelers passing through. The smell of freshly baked bread wafted across the stalls from the hot stoneware ovens. Dried fish hung from wires strung across the stalls, and brown eggs, fresh tomatoes, and other vegetables were piled randomly on the tables. Dust and flies covered everything.

Known as Lake Nubia in Sudan, Lake Nasser mostly lies in Egypt. Built as a reservoir by the Egyptians with Russian financing in 1967, the lake was designed to control the annual Nile floods and generate hydroelectric power. Unfortunately, the reservoir construction caused many environmental problems, buried several Egyptian temples, and displaced thousands of Nubian people.

There was no passable land-border crossing from Sudan to Egypt

for foreigners, so we had to arrange boat transport up the lake to
Egypt. At Wadi Halfa, we met up with two other couples in vehicles
heading to Egypt—a British couple, Robert and Jenny, and Don and
Isabelle from Spain. We decided we'd try to cross the lake together.

The logistics of this crossing posed a challenge, especially because
vehicles were involved. Ferry service was weekly, and cargo, including
vehicles, went separately. We heard that a privately contracted cement
barge was returning to Egypt the following week and had space on
board for four vehicles. In this situation, we could remain with our
vehicles, something not possible if we used the regular passenger
ferry. Negotiations and the inevitable paperwork began. Then, after
the vehicles were measured, customs cleared, documents processed,
and payment made, the barge was scheduled to leave in five days with
all of us on board. We should have been apprehensive, as we hadn't
even seen the barge when we agreed on a price. But as was often the
case on our journey, events moved quickly, and we had to make decisions fast just to keep up.

For the next five nights, we camped in a sheltered location, with
towering dunes on one side and the blue waters of Lake Nubia on the
other. Fishermen gave us some of their daily catch, and camel herders
grazed their camels on the sparse vegetation close to the shore. I slept
fitfully under the stars, and in the sunlight, alone with my thoughts, I
wandered across the sandy dunes and into the solitude of the Sahara
Desert. I contemplated, cried, and agonized, trying to make sense of
all that had happened. I could still feel the boy's mother's tears on my
cheeks and hear his father's cries. But their courageous compassion
and forgiveness revealed their humanity and ours. It reminded me of
the African word *Ubuntu*: "I am because of you"—we can only find
our humanity in relationships with others. Our journey had shown
Tom and me that we could truly trust and depend on each other in
the most challenging and tragic of times. Our humanity toward each
other and strangers had been realized. I looked up at the cloudless sky,

and a sense of gratitude that Tom was at my side on the journey welled up in me. I knew then that if I had made this trip alone, Tom and I would have missed out on learning the most important lesson in our lives: the essence of every meaningful and loving relationship is to be fully present with each other. We had unshackled ourselves from how we used to be in each other's lives and the world. We had found each other again. We had reclaimed our *Ubuntu*.

On our last night at the camp, the night sky was clear, and the flames in our firepit danced in the warm, gentle breeze. We all began packing up and preparing for loading onto the barge in the morning. I walked up to Tom, who was in the car, calibrating our GPS for Egypt.

"Where's the stone you gave me at the beginning of our trip at Cape Point?" I asked. "The one I wrote 'Cairo or Bust' on."

He leaned over and retrieved the round gray stone from the glove compartment. "What are you going to do with it?"

The stone rested in the palm of my hand. Like my life, even the stone had changed on this journey. The crudely written words, 'Cairo or Bust,' were now hard to read due to the scratches. I was no longer the same person who had left Cape Town. The essence of my being had crossed a line in the desert. I thought about all the times I had disappointed myself because I had not achieved a goal I set for myself or my relationships—dreams never realized. I began to understand that life doesn't happen according to my plans and goals. Life happens. Tom and I should expect to be thrown off course, plunge into deep and dark ravines, and stand on the tops of glorious mountains we didn't even know existed. And we should meet strangers, who might shower us with kindness or challenge us with scams and threats.

"I now know that Cairo was never meant to be my destination. I had something more important ahead when we left Cape Town."

He smiled. "You got that right."

I walked down to the water's edge. "I am letting you go," I

whispered, and I dropped the stone into the Nile waters. It disappeared beneath a wave of ripples.

I was about to begin one of the most difficult journeys of my life. The death of the child had gutted me with grief and guilt. I would have to learn to navigate through the anguish I felt. I had to go through it. I could not detour around it. I would have to breathe into my struggles and learn to let go. Was that even possible?

I felt Tom put his arm around me. "You threw that stone into the river, right?" he asked.

I trembled as I nodded my head. "Yes."

"You did the right thing. We could never have known our destination was never meant to be Cairo."

Finally, Thursday dawned, and we arrived at the shipping office at 8:30 a.m. to begin the process of boarding the barge. At 2:00 p.m., the officials instructed us to proceed to the harbor. We arrived at the loading dock, and our collective jaws dropped when we saw the vessel.

Rusted and covered in gray cement dust, it had no safety railing and was barely wide enough to fit a vehicle. The toilet consisted of a metal bucket at the barge's stern with an unobstructed, 360-degree view. In the center of the barge was a large gaping hole through which they put the cargo to be stored below deck. The young barge captain, in cement-dust-covered, oil-stained pants and shirt, instructed us to park two vehicles on each side of the gaping hole. The barge was about four feet from the dock, so the crew placed two rickety wooden planks, barely wide enough for a wheel, between the dock and the barge as a vehicle ramp. One slip and the Cruiser would end up in the lake. After much intense discussion and negotiations among the four men, Tom said he would go first.

I threw my arms up in the air. "Tom, this is crazy! You don't even have functioning brakes. If you even make it onto the barge, you'll end up going off the other side." My heart beat wildly at the thought of Tom plunging into the water.

He quietly reassured me he could do it and handed me our passports, important documents, computer, and cameras. He got into the car and rolled down the car windows so he could escape from the Cruiser if it fell into the water. I felt I would break.

The barge crew and other men who gathered to watch the loading knelt and, facing Mecca, prayed on the dockside. I turned around, unable to watch.

I heard Don helping Tom line up each wheel with one of the wood planks: "A little to the left; too much. Go slightly right. Okay, stop!"

"The wheels lined up properly?" Tom asked. I imagined him leaning out of the window.

"Okay, you're good to go. Slowly now," Don instructed.

The wooden planks creaked and groaned under the strain as the wheels crept up them. The engine hummed. The seagulls screeched above. Nobody made a sound. Then I heard the screams. "He's on. He's made it!"

I spun around. The front of the Cruiser nearly protruded over the starboard side of the barge, the back bumper in line with the port side. Tom had only inches to spare. He got out of the Cruiser, a smile of success across his face. "Three more vehicles to go," he announced, wiping the sweat off his brow with the back of his hand.

Finally, with all four vehicles on board, secured only by hand brakes and sturdy ropes that we'd supplied, our journey toward the Egyptian border began. As the barge ventured out of port, it shuddered, creaked, and groaned as the waves slapped its sides. I sat down, as I hadn't yet found my sea legs on the unstable vessel. The last vehicle blocked access to the battered metal bucket at the stern, so we either had to crawl under or go through the cab of Marc's truck to reach the bucket toilet.

"This is going to be a scary journey," I remarked.

"I'm not sure we'll survive the damn thing," Tom replied. He pulled on the rope holding our Cruiser. "These ropes better hold. And I hope we don't sail into a storm."

As the crew steered out into the waters of Lake Nubia, everybody began to set up their gear, a process that turned out to be trickier than we'd thought it would be. There was too much wind for us to put up our rooftop tent, and getting access to the rear of our Cruiser was a death-defying act.

Meanwhile, a second barge had pulled alongside us, and its crew lassoed it with ropes to our barge. The gap between the two barges was just large enough for a person to slip overboard and never be seen again. Waves splashed over the deck and soaked everything.

I shook my head. "I can't believe we're doing this."

"I'm beginning to think that too," Tom murmured.

I hung on to the car. "*Inshallah*—God willing—we'll make it."

Chapter 19
Seven Hundred Miles to Cairo

Egypt, 2006

The scenery and starlit nights made up for our primitive and precarious living conditions. The miles slipped away. The surrounding desert shorelines changed from soft yellows to hazy pinks as the sun moved across the sky. The Egyptian Abu Simbel temples eventually appeared in the distance. The colossal statues of the pharaohs sculptured directly into the pink rock wall of the mountain cast long shadows in the late-afternoon sun. Staring at the ghostly shadows while the boat swayed and creaked lulled me into a hypnotic state.

On Saturday morning, the port of Aswan in Egypt came into view. After two sleepless nights and three days of sailing, we were all exhausted, filthy, and covered with gray cement dust. We looked like ghosts and smelled so bad even the flies avoided us.

Cargo and fishing boats, ferries, and barges, all in a state of disrepair and neglect, blocked access to the grubby port. Boats were anchored alongside one another so tightly that there was no place for our cement barge to dock. With tensions running high and shouts in Arabic, the men on our barge and those on the dockside fought. Our barge continued going until it rammed a boat, at which point our captain repositioned the barge and rammed another boat again and again. Our Cruiser swayed, tugging against the ropes. The men on our barge jumped across to the other boat. Amid protests and shouting, they untied that boat from its anchoring. Our captain rammed the other vessel repeatedly until he'd managed to wedge his barge between it and the dockside.

Our crew scrambled to tie up our barge, yelling at Tom to get the Cruiser off immediately. Because there were no ramps, they expected Tom to move the vehicle by reversing it off the cement barge at high speed across the gap between the barge and the dockside. Since the barge was lower than the dockside, Tom would need to give enough power to launch the Cruiser by hitting the gunwale of the barge and bouncing the vehicle up and over the low barrier and onto the dock. The men discussed the risk that the force of a vehicle striking the jetty would push the barge farther away from the dockside. Our Cruiser would then fall into the water and become a fixture of the port of Aswan. I stood there in disbelief at what was about to happen.

"We can't be here. We must get the cars off quickly," the crew shouted at Tom as they began to untie the ropes holding the Cruiser onto the barge.

Tom was furious. "I will not be rushed. This is fucking dangerous, and my car is heavy." He stood with his hands on his head as if trying to come up with a better idea.

"We have to move before the boat owner returns," the crew replied, referring to the boat they had pushed away.

"That's not my problem. This is unsafe, and I will do it when I'm damn ready."

Our group discussed the dangerous situation again and instructed our captain to move the barge slightly forward. After the final push, Tom was ready to reverse the car off the barge. Don provided direction because Tom couldn't see where he was going out of the back window or the rearview mirror of the Cruiser, which was packed with camping gear and other equipment. I held my breath, but this time I watched. Tom climbed into the car, and everyone fell silent. The crew and the dockworkers knelt in prayer. Tom turned on the ignition, and the engine roared to life. A crowd on the dockside gathered to watch, their silence making the situation more nerve-racking.

"You're looking good," Don said. "You ready?"

"I'm ready," Tom replied. "Remember, I can't see anything out the back."

"Now!" Don shouted.

Tom gave full acceleration. The Cruiser roared. The crowd burst into screams: "Go. Go. Go!"

Suddenly our Cruiser's wheels smashed against the jetty. The Cruiser bounced and then, with full power, shot over the barrier— Tom had landed on the dockside. Cheers rang out, and there were many congratulations. However, the task wasn't over; we still had three more vehicles to disembark. The captain had to maneuver the barge for each one. The process was agonizing and slow. Finally, the last vehicle to disembark was safely on land.

With the complicated task of disembarking completed, a customs official escorted us from the dockside into Immigration and Customs. There we were whisked into the office of the dreaded "Mr. Carnet," rumored to be difficult and obsessive about carnet details, unlike his counterparts at other borders. Sitting behind a desk with paper scattered across it, Mr. Carnet waved his arm, indicating to us to sit on the bench along his office wall. He wore a navy jacket and a white open-neck shirt. Chest hairs peeped over the top button. He was middle-aged, with short curly black hair and a complexion the color of desert sand. His bushy eyebrows seemed to peer over his thick glasses, which were balanced precariously on the tip of his nose.

We handed over our documents. His dark eyes hardened with a bureaucratic authority, and his brow furrowed. It remained that way for the hour he spent reviewing the documents. Before turning each page, he licked the tip of his right index finger. He stopped only once and made himself some tea while eight dusty, exhausted travelers watched silently. We all knew he had one forged carnet document in his hands—Don and Isabelle had had no other options at one of their border crossings earlier in their trip, and they had told us about the forgery. I shuddered, imagining the scene if Mr. Carnet discovered it.

We each had an opinion on whether it was good enough to stand his scrutiny.

Mr. Carnet completed and stamped forms with a whack and continued to read each document—a painfully slow process. I began to suspect that his thick wire-rimmed glasses perhaps meant that he couldn't see well. *Can he see the forged details?* I wondered. I glanced over at Tom. Our eyes met, then darted between Mr. Carnet, the documents, and each other. Our silent conversation. Tom nodded, and I relaxed.

Finally, Mr. Carnet returned our carnets. Immigration stamped our passports and cleared us for entrance into Egypt. But we were not permitted to take our vehicles out of the port until we had Egyptian insurance, license plates, and driver's licenses. So, we all bundled into a black-and-white Peugeot cab and headed to the town to obtain all the requirements to release our vehicles.

Three days later, we returned to the port. The port authorities instructed us to drill holes into our license plates to attach our Egyptian plates. But we all refused and instead attached them with duct tape and wire. Now, only a cursory police check was required.

I soon learned that there was no such thing as a cursory Egyptian police check. The policemen told us to unpack our vehicles so they could be searched. Exhausted and in no mood to unpack anything, especially since it would take us hours to unpack and repack, we all refused. Heated arguments flared up with lots of gesticulating, confusion, frustration, and yelling on both sides until Mr. Carnet arrived on the scene. He explained that the police had to search everything in case we were carrying bombs.

"Bombs!" Tom exclaimed. "We don't have any damn bombs, and we're not unpacking." The others agreed. We were so tightly packed that I wondered where we could have put bombs. Unable to convince any of us to cooperate, Mr. Carnet shrugged, pushed his wire glasses up his nose, and walked away.

Finally, in desperation, a policeman disappeared to discuss the situation with his supervisor. The supervisor returned shortly afterward with the policeman. He briefly looked over the vehicles, nodded, and said we were free to leave.

The British may have invented bureaucracy, but the Egyptians have perfected it. Fifty-two forms and three days later, they granted us permission to leave the port. We got into our vehicles and headed to the exit gate.

A young port attendant directed us to pull over to the side of the road. "You pay $3 for parking," he said.

After all the hassles, costs, and three days of bureaucracy at its worst, Robert snapped. "You made us stay here. I'm not paying for damn parking!"

Don and Mark got out of their vehicles. The attendant stepped back, stood quietly for a minute, unsure what to do, and then repeated his request.

Don raised his fist. "You heard him. We're not paying."

"Oh, shit," Tom mumbled, and he got out of the Cruiser. He walked over to join the men. With the commotion getting louder, a senior-looking port official arrived. Don informed him we would block the entrance and exit to the port with our four vehicles until they let us go.

"Get behind me," he said to our group. "We're in this together." The men returned to their vehicles without a word and started them up. I looked out the window. A crowd of onlookers had gathered.

"We've all gone insane," I said as our group parked their vehicles to block the port entrance and exit.

"I know," Tom nodded. "And the real danger is that everything will spin out of our control."

"Then why are we doing this?"

"We need to stick together." He paused. "The only power we have now is in our numbers."

More police arrived. I imagined our arrests, the headlines about the incident, but I was too tired to care. Truckers began furiously honking their horns. Despite heated, loud discussions, our trav-el-weary men refused to pay or move our vehicles.

"It's your fault. You made us park here," was the repeated message that the men gave to the equally frustrated officials and police.

"Travelers from the south all much trouble. Very difficult," explained one port official to the police. I glanced at Tom and the others: we all looked wild and a little threatening. A senior official walked toward our parked vehicles blocking the port entrance. He said something to the police and port officials and left. Surprised, I watched the red-and-white exit boom rise.

"Go," said an official.

Tom put on his sunglasses and started up the Cruiser.

"Tom, do you think this international parking protest will come back to haunt us?" I asked.

"We'll just have to wait and see." He rolled down his window. "But right now, all I want is to be out of this damn port,"

That evening, we celebrated our entry into Aswan, Egypt, with sunset drinks on the porch of the Old Cataract Hotel, where Agatha Christie stayed while writing her book *Death on the Nile*. The venue was most appropriate, given that our own Nile experience had nearly been the death of us.

Once a little fishing village, Aswan was now a port of call for large river-cruise boats, which sailed down the Nile River to Abu Simbel in southern Egypt. While the Cruiser's brakes were getting fixed, Tom and I spent time wandering through the colorful souk—the open-air markets where vendors hustled tourists to buy aromatic spices, fresh vegetables and fruit, kitschy souvenirs, and semiprecious stones.

Jostled by well-heeled tourists, busy locals, and eager salespeople, I finally turned to Tom and said, "I can't be around all these people. I just can't."

"Me too." He took my hand. "Let's get out of here."

We walked toward the Nile, passing horse carriages with tourists. Eager young tour guides hassled us: "Cheap but very good tour. You come with me." I wanted to disappear, to be left alone. Tom and I picked up our pace until we were out of the noisy bustle of the town center.

We sat on the riverbank in the shade of a palm tree. Small birds chattered in the branches above. In the distance, feluccas (traditional wooden sailing boats) glided, without a sound, across the waters.

I sat in silence, trapped in a web of confusing thoughts and shattered by the unresolved issue of my guilt around the accident. I still saw the child's horrified face each time I looked at the bull bar he had clutched before disappearing from my sight.

"I'm struggling to make sense of all that happened," I said.

Tom breathed in deeply and let out a long sigh. "I can still feel the fear I felt when I thought you might go to prison."

He put his arm around me and pulled me closer. Tears flowed, and I wiped my snotty nose with the back of my arm.

We sat quietly for a while before returning to pick up our Cruiser.

"We should take a longer route to Cairo," Tom suggested. "It'll give us time to be by ourselves, to process everything, before returning home."

I agreed. Our most meaningful times together were while alone in the Cruiser. It had become our sanctuary, our place of quiet meditation, of rowdy discussions, laughter, and tears.

That evening we decided to go to Abu Simbel. We estimated it would take about three hours to get there, and the following morning we headed south. Several hours later, we stood at the base of four colossal, enthroned statues that dominate the entrance of the thirteenth-century Great Temple of Abu Simbel, built to honor Ramses II.

The pink rocks glowed in the warm sun. I reflected on how complex and fragile cultures are due to the loss of ancient knowledge, traditions, and unique understandings of the world, which lie buried in the sands of the earth. I thought about how complex and fragile Tom's and my relationship had been when we'd set off for Cairo. In the beginning, I'd doubted that our relationship would survive; we had drifted so far apart. I had wondered if it was even possible to rediscover what we first loved about each other. Now when I looked across at Tom, I no longer could imagine him not being part of my life.

As the day drew to an end, the stars started to expose themselves, eventually forming that always-fresh masterpiece of nature—a starry night sky. I climbed up into our tent and lay down but struggled to sleep.

In the morning, with the sun just peeking over the horizon, we packed up and headed north for Cairo, seven hundred miles away.

I picked up our Egypt map and opened it on my lap. I traced my finger along small side roads heading north and thought of all the route decisions we had made on our journey. We never knew what lay ahead, no matter which track or road we chose. Each day we ventured into the unpredictable and unknown, which we grew to love—not knowing what we would see and experience or the people who would touch our lives and, most importantly, the lessons they would teach us.

I thought of the woman in the coffin in Tanzania who made me realize my journey was not about reaching Cairo. The mechanics in Zambia who told us that white people don't have to like one another because they don't have to rely on one another. The priest who had blessed us in Botswana, and his followers who graciously shared their bread and water with us. The Malawian who made a bolt by hand, reminding us of the loss of craftsmanship in the new world. I especially thought of the dead child's mother, Enatelem. Working as a pediatric nurse, I had seen children die, but no child's death had brought me closer to the pain of a mother losing a child. Through her generosity of kindness toward me, she taught me one of the most important lessons of my life: the wisdom of compassion and forgiveness.

Despite the guilt I still carried—and always would—about the little boy's death, I somehow began to accept that the tragedy had opened the possibility for a more in-depth, more meaningful exploration for both Tom and me of our lives and our relationships.

Chapter 20

A Second Chance at
Life and Relationship

Egypt, 2006

Wind blew through the open windows, and a small beaded gecko ornament that hung on the passenger side of the Cruiser's windshield danced in the breeze. A chewed ballpoint pen hung from a piece of string attached to the passenger door. A notepad rested on the dashboard. Bug spray, maps, guidebooks, flashlights, and sunscreen were stuffed into the door side pockets. All of these things were strangely comforting, old friends that helped me to settle in for long drives. I listened to the sound of our Cruiser's engine on the faithful vehicle's final journey with us.

I gazed out the car window at the desolate landscape as we drove the strip of road north toward White Desert National Park—a wild landscape of eroded chalk and limestone rocks. Wind and erosion sculptured the mysterious white rocks over the years into large, mystical shapes: glistening mushrooms, sphinxes, and other formations. As the sun set, the white chalk hoodoos took on pink, orange, and yellow hues—a snowy-looking winter in Africa.

That night through the open tent door, I watched the busy carpet of planets and millions of stars in the heavens above on this, our final night before heading into Cairo. I never imagined our travels would take me on a journey of discoveries, not only about the world but about me, about us. I listened to Tom's soft snore. I reached out and touched his hair, all with some comfort. Perhaps part of the emptiness I had felt in my life was the absence of a deep and meaningful relationship between Tom and me. We had filled our lives with children, careers, distractions, and stuff, and in the busyness, we had lost sight of each other. We had lived parallel lives, each on our own track.

A haze hung over the traffic-logged, noisy city of Cairo. Drivers seemed to disregard road signs, one-way streets, traffic lights, or lines on the roads. The traffic was anarchy. We pulled in our side mirrors to avoid having them smashed by cars passing too close. The constant blaring of horns added to the chaos.

I glanced at two Bedouin men riding camels as I drove passed them. "We need to find somewhere to stay tonight," I said.

Tom glanced at our GPS. "I'll watch for a sign. Just keep going. We'll find somewhere."

It wasn't long before he saw a sign for hotels. "Okay," he said, "turn right at the corner."

I weaved through the traffic, following Tom's instructions. Soon several hotels came into sight, and in the distance stood the three pyramids. When we left Cape Town, I had anticipated the enormous excitement I would feel when we reached Cairo, but I only felt a quiet sense of relief. "We've made it safely," I said.

That evening we headed to a rooftop patio of a hotel overlooking the pyramids. A young waiter showed us to a table with a view, poured some coffee into glass mugs, and gave us each a menu. Music from the outdoor patio fought to be heard above the traffic sounds in the streets below.

"I don't want to ship from Egypt," Tom said, shaking his head. "I can just imagine the bureaucratic paperwork involved in that. I think we should head to Israel and ship the Cruiser from there. It'll be quicker and easier." Because of the carnet document, the Cruiser had to be legally shipped back to South Africa, where it was registered.

I stirred my coffee, which released a nutty aroma hinting of cardamom. "Okay" was all I could muster.

Over the next few days, we arranged for the car to be serviced and for some bodywork to be done, and we researched the logistics of shipping the Cruiser back to Cape Town.

Several days later, we packed up, ready to leave and face the chaos of Cairo traffic once again. Tom turned on our music, and we listened to Vivaldi as we drove into the darkness of the tunnel under the Suez Canal and out into the sunshine of the windswept, ochre-colored rocky desert of the Sinai Peninsula.

As we arrived at the village of Dahab, the sun had just begun to set over the deep-turquoise tropical waters of the Red Sea. Later we wandered down to the sandy beach, lined with open-air, Bedouin-style restaurants. Sipping fruit juices and beers, locals and tourists in bathing suits lounged on colorful deck chairs draped with wet towels and wetsuits. Stray cats and dogs waited for scraps, and seagulls rested on the signposts. Melodic Arabic music beat out from speakers, and the aromas of spicy evening meals wafted over the crowds.

In the warm evening breeze, we walked away from the crowd and found a quiet spot on the beach. Lights from sailboats and dive boats twinkled in the distance. The night sky blazed with stars. A deep sadness swept over me. I thought of all I would miss.

Most of all, I would miss the closeness of Tom, our laughs, agreements, analysis, and arguments every moment of every day. We had brought out the best and the worst in each other and discovered a new way of being in the world and each other's lives. We had found each other; we had found the third persona in our marriage, the "us." Of course, I never could have imagined that it would take a horrific tragedy to pull us together. But in the depth of our vulnerabilities, we had found the strength and trust to totally depend on each other.

A slight breeze stirred the grains of sand. Tom built a small campfire, and we sat alone in the glow. The hours passed.

"I'm going to miss this life," I admitted quietly, thinking of the sound of the earth crunching beneath the foot of an elephant, the calls of birds at dawn, the smoke of charcoal fires drifting across the valleys at the end of the day, and of all the strangers who had welcomed us into their lives. And the night sky of stars—I would miss the millions of stars.

"Me too." Tom's voice sounded soft and unhurried.

Israel, March 2006

It was early morning when we arrived at the Israel border. The female official approached Tom and asked for our passports, documents, and the reasons for our coming to Israel. After several minutes, she returned our documents and welcomed us to Israel.

It was clear from the minute we drove into Eilat, Israel's most southern resort town on the Gulf, that we were back in the modern world. Not since leaving Cape Town had we seen so much affluence. Traffic lights worked, stores were filled with luxury items, and people looked well-fed and healthy everywhere. We parked, got out, and strolled along the beachfront. We bought falafels and cokes at a food stand and sat to have our lunch on a low brick wall.

The sea breeze felt good on my face, the beach sand warm between my toes, and I could taste the salt of the air. All around us, tanned teenagers in skimpy bathing suits lay on the beach, chatting and listening to their music. Engrossed in a book, an older woman sat beneath a blue-and-yellow-striped umbrella. Laughing children ran down the beach, holding on to their kites, which trailed behind them high in the sky.

I glanced at Tom. He looked as wild as the waves on the beach. I imagined him back at home, his untamed beard gone, his hair trimmed, tan faded, and his jacket and tie slung over the back of a chair. I wiggled my toes into the sand and said, "Every day for the past eight months, we never knew what the day ahead held, and I've never felt more alive, more energized."

Tom sighed. "Yeah. It's been quite the journey."

Friends in a village near Tel Aviv invited us to stay with them. Their home served as our base for packing the Cruiser and other items for shipping. Our room soon became an obstacle course as the contents of some fifteen boxes and bags were spilled onto the floor for sorting. A few days later, with all our luggage packed, we thanked them for their hospitality and headed for the Port of Ashdod, an hour away, to ship the Cruiser back to South Africa.

Tom drove while I navigated. I watched as we passed farmers working in the fields and shoppers carrying bags in the villages, and I thought of all we'd gone through.

Our relationship, like the dunes of the Sahara, had continuously shifted and changed during our travels. I couldn't ignore the seismic shifts we had undergone. Exposed to the outside world, we, as a couple, had witnessed, learned, and experienced more than we ever could have imagined. We discovered a world of both wonderment and complexities. My perspective about myself and Tom changed. And I learned to love all over again Tom's compassion and gentleness, the firmness and strength he displayed on our journey, especially in Ethiopia, when I needed him most.

At the port, a balding middle-aged man directed us to a loading dock where an empty twenty-foot shipping container stood. It was a tight fit, but soon our Cruiser was in. After we secured the vehicle, the container was closed, locked, and sealed, and our home on wheels was gone. After traveling twenty-five thousand miles through many countries—and even a couple of centuries—I felt I was saying goodbye to a best friend and to a way of life that begged me to stay.

I was concerned that we would slip back into our old patterns and habits of urban monotony. Instead of roosters or songbirds, alarm clocks would wake us in the mornings. The smells of the earth would lie hidden beneath neat gardens, roads, buildings, or shoveled pathways. We'd want for nothing. The daily struggles to survive would be gone, but with them, the adrenaline rushes. My compressed energies would pound through my body, with few escape routes. I knew that I would struggle to rejoin our sanitized life. Only when life hurled challenges at me did I learn the lessons I needed to guide and make me a better, more compassionate person.

A cab driver picked us up at the port and drove us to Tel Aviv on the shores of the Mediterranean Sea. An hour later, we stopped in front of a small hotel where, in both directions, palm trees in planters lined the sidewalk.

The small hotel room had two clean beds, a shower with hot water, and a toilet that flushed. I sat on the bed and removed my sandals, but before I could lie down, Tom suggested we go for supper.

Locals chatted, sipped wine, and laughed in the sidewalk café. Tom ordered a lamb shish kebab. I said I wasn't hungry. The sounds of a city that never sleeps—traffic, music, people—filled the crisp evening air, and city lights illuminated the evening sky.

"I want to hold on to the new and vital life we've found," I said.

He sat quietly for several minutes, then said, "Africa has opened my mind, heart, and soul to a different way of being in the world. I feel I've—" he looked at me, "—we've been given a second chance at both life and our relationship."

"I feel like we're teetering on the edge of a new way of being in the world," I said.

Tom leaned back. "Remember when we left on our journey, you said that our marriage therapy had only thrown us life jackets and we were no longer drowning, but we still had to swim to shore?" He reached out and put his hand on my arm. "I think we've reached that shore."

We sat quietly together. There were times when I had drifted peacefully toward shore, and other times, I felt I was drowning in the currents of life. To keep my head above the waves, I had to let go of everything that weighed me down: regrets, resentments, disappointments, and tragedies in life. The memory of Getaw's death and his mother's compassion and forgiveness had given me the strength to reach the shore and the courage to face life's realities.

The following morning, the hum of a city waking and the glow of the morning sun through the open window woke me. Tom was already sitting up in bed.

"I've been waiting for you to wake up," he said. "I'll get you some coffee. The cab to the airport will be here in an hour."

Two hours later, we arrived at Ben Gurion International Airport. After we had checked our luggage through and were processed through customs and immigration, we retreated to a restaurant. I was tired, hot, and filled with sadness at leaving Africa, the continent that had breathed so much life back into me and into our relationship. Music playing in the restaurant pulsed through my body. Finally, our El Al flight was called.

"Come," said Tom, "it's time to head home."

Epilogue

Tom and I are truly grateful for the diverse richness of our cultural experiences; they shifted our perceptions about the world, humanity, and ourselves. After we returned to Canada and shared our experiences, the most frequent question people asked was, "How did you two put up with each other alone in a car for hundreds of days?"

The journey had been challenging. We cried, we argued, but mostly we laughed. While on the road alone, we slowly unpeeled our relationship, digging deeper and deeper until the invisible became visible. We laid ourselves bare and navigated through the emotional terrain of our marriage, identifying the roadblocks that held us back, and the landmines that blew us apart. We stepped out from the uncertainty and fragility of our marriage. We went from breakdown to breakthrough.

We left for our Cape-to-Cairo expedition with a million questions and returned with another million. Our curiosity about the world was set on fire, and on our return, we were soon planning again. Before we sold our Land Cruiser, we returned to Africa to complete two more extensive overland expeditions across West Africa. In 2010, we sold everything, bought a truck camper, and drove from Alaska to Argentina.

At the time of writing this book, the mother of the child who died, Getaw, had given birth to two more children. Understandably, the father said no child would ever replace his eldest son. The grieving mother's kindness and forgiveness had a powerful impact on me, and I will carry her wisdom of compassion forever.

Amanual, our translator, who helped us with the translation, with documents, and with dealing with officials, told us that the government had just stated that official tour guides required a mandatory two-year tour-guide course. We sponsored Amanual's education, and he qualified as an official tour guide.

We offered Anteneh, the nurse at the village who showed us so much kindness, the opportunity to upgrade his education. He now works for the Ministry of Health in Ethiopia.

Acknowledgments

It's been years writing this memoir, and many people helped me on my journey.

Tom: Thank you for your courage, trust, and love, especially during the challenges of our travels and my writing journey. You are a beautiful soul.

Derek and David: Thank you for your unconditional love and support, especially during our travels.

Olive Senior: Thank you for your guidance and wisdom with my first draft, and for helping me find my voice and encouraging me to keep writing.

Tim Bowling: What can I say but that you are the best editor I could have wished for. A mentor who pushed me into the depth of my writing. Thank you, Tim.

I am grateful for the many writers-in-residence and authors who offer me gems of wisdom, encouragement, and support. Thank you Marcello Di Cintio, Louise Bernice Halfe, Bradley Sommer, Lee Kvern, Steven Ross Smith, John Valliant, Omar Mouallem, Teresa Wong, Micheline Maylor, Ali Bryan, Rona Altrows, and many others.

About the Author

photo credit: Jillian Faulkner

Janet A. Wilson is a South Africa–born author and adventurer with a passion for Africa's wilderness, wildlife, and diverse cultures. She met her husband, Tom, during student anti-apartheid protests in South Africa, and they later immigrated to Canada with their sons in 1979. Together, they have completed three extensive overland travels, driving a total of over 50,000 miles around Africa as well as from Alaska to Argentina and around Europe. Janet has a degree in sociology and nursing and obtained her master's in health administration. She completed the Creative Nonfiction Certificate Course at Toronto's Humber School of Writers. She and Tom currently live in Calgary, Canada.

SELECTED TITLES FROM SHE WRITES PRESS

She Writes Press is an independent publishing company founded to serve women writers everywhere. Visit us at www.shewritespress.com.

Brave(ish): A Memoir of a Recovering Perfectionist by Margaret Davis Ghielmetti. $16.95, 978-1-63152-747-0

An intrepid traveler sets off at forty to live the expatriate dream over-seas—only to discover that she has no idea how to live even her own life. Part travelogue and part transformation tale, Ghielmetti's memoir, narrated with humor and warmth, proves that it's never too late to reconnect with our authentic selves—if we dare to put our own lives first at last.

Bowing to Elephants: Tales of a Travel Junkie by Mag Dimond $16.95, 978-1-63152-596-4

Mag Dimond, an unloved girl from San Francisco, becomes a travel junkie to avoid the fate of her narcissistic, alcoholic mother—but every-where she goes, she's haunted by memories of her mother's neglect, and by a hunger to find out who she is, until she finds peace and her authentic self in the refuge of Buddhist practice.

Finding Venerable Mother: A Daughter's Spiritual Quest to Thailand by Cindy Rasicot. $16.95, 978-1-63152-702-9

In midlife, Cindy travels halfway around the world to Thailand and unex-pectedly discovers a Thai Buddhist nun who offers her the unconditional love and acceptance her own mother was never able to provide. This soul-ful and engaging memoir reminds readers that when we go forward with a truly open heart, faith, forgiveness, and love are all possible.

Just Be: A Search for Self-Love in India by Meredith Rom $16.95, 978-1-63152-286-4

After following her intuition to fly across the world and travel alone through the crowded streets of India, twenty-two-year-old Meredith Rom learns that that true spiritual development begins when we take the leap of trusting our intuition and finding a love within.